Treatment of the Masochistic Personality

Treatment of the Masochistic Personality

An Interactional-Object Relations Approach to Psychotherapy

Cheryl Glickauf-Hughes, Ph.D.
and
Marolyn Wells, Ph.D.

JASON ARONSON INC.
Northvale, New Jersey
London

The authors gratefully acknowledge permission to reprint the following:

Material from "Current Conceptualizations of Masochism: Genesis and Object Relations," by Cheryl Glickauf-Hughes and Marolyn Wells, in the *American Journal of Psychotherapy*, vol. 45, no. 1, pp. 53–68. Copyright © 1991 by the Association for the Advancement of Psychotherapy. Used by permission.

Material from "Dynamics and Treatment of the Masochistic-Narcissistic Couple," by Cheryl Glickauf-Hughes, in *Psychoanalysis and Psychotherapy*, vol. 11, no. 1, pp. 32–44. Copyright © 1994 by International Universities Press. Used by permission.

Production Editor: Elaine Lindenblatt

This book was set in 10 point Bookman by TechType of Upper Saddle River, New Jersey, and printed and bound by Haddon Craftsmen of Scranton, Pennsylvania.

Library of Congress Cataloging-in-Publication Data

Glickauf-Hughes, Cheryl.
    Treatment of the masochistic personality : an interactional-object relations approach to psychotherapy / by Cheryl Glickauf-Hughes and Marolyn Wells.
        p. cm.
    Includes bibliographical references and index.
    ISBN 1-56821-384-0
    1. Masochism—Treatment. 2. Psychotherapy. 3. Object relations (Psychoanalysis) I. Wells, Marolyn Clark. II. Title.
    RC553.M36G56   1995
    616.85′835—dc20
                                                        94-34953

Manufactured in the United States of America. Jason Aronson Inc. offers books and cassettes. For information and catalog write to Jason Aronson Inc., 230 Livingston Street, Northvale, New Jersey 07647.

To George and Richard

Contents

Acknowledgments

The authors wish to express appreciation to those individuals who have proven to be special mentors in our lives: John M. Nardo, Billie Ables, William Mueller, Pauline Clance, Doug Miller, Zander Ponzo, Josiah Dilley, and Marcelle Teitler. The wisdom and the encouragement that we have gained from our relationships with these individuals have contributed immeasurably to this work.

Of equal importance, the authors thank the many clients whose lives and struggles we have been permitted to share and from whom we have learned much. Witnessing so many determined individuals attempt to overcome difficult childhood relationships and self-defeating adaptations, only to reach seemingly insurmountable impasses, inspired us to learn more about the development and treatment of masochism.

We would also like to thank our colleagues and students for their critical evaluation of this work. In particular, the feedback of Owen Renik, Susan Chance, Nivine Megahed, Robert Simmermon, John Paddock, Luciano L'Abate, and Nicolette Scofield has greatly helped us to refine our concepts. We would also like to acknowledge Sonja Gardner and Susan Campbell for their superb job of typing and preparing this manuscript.

1

Introduction

Masochism has become, over time, one of the most confusing and controversial clinical and diagnostic terms within the psychotherapy literature. One reason for this debate is that, historically, masochism has been equated with that which is feminine or female (e.g., Bardwick 1971, Deutsch 1944, Freud 1924, 1919, Gero 1962, Horney 1939, Krafft-Ebbing 1895) and has been defined in terms of the victim's enjoyment of and need for pain.

As Gero (1962) noted, "Sadistic acts are identified with the role of the male who is depicted as the cruel attacker who inflicts pain and injury. The masochistic destiny is viewed as woman's lot. She endures cruel acts and finds pleasure in yielding and submission" (p. 31). Due to the prevalence of associating this delimited definition of masochism with women, critics have objected to the term as sexist and victim-blaming (Caplan 1984). Feminists, in particular, "see it as a dangerous weapon that could frequently be misused to blame women, particularly abused women, for societal failures" (Franklin 1987, p. 53).

On the other hand, a substantial segment of the therapeutic community—particularly, although not limited to the psychoanalytic sector (i.e., Beck 1967, Glick and Meyers 1988) still avidly claims that this diagnosis offers an important tool for identifying individuals with excessive, chronic, and repetitive self-sabotaging proclivities (Franklin 1987). For such advocates the misapplications of this diagnosis do not negate its essential validity, just as the historical misuses of the histrionic (hysterical) and sociopathic constructs did not invalidate their clinical reality or usefulness. Proponents of masochism esteem the explanatory value of the construct in the clinical setting and believe that it denotes a character pathology "that seems endemic to our culture and is a common motivation for patients to seek treatment" (Asch 1988, p. 100).

As a temporary compromise between the protests against and the defenses of this diagnosis, the American Psychiatric Association (APA) determined that their diagnostic manual (*DSM-III-R*, APA 1987) would exclude this personality disorder from its official listings but would include in the appendix the transformed and possibly less inflammatory rubric of self-defeating personality disorder. This inclusion was accompanied by a call for further study and consideration of this disorder in order to help the APA determine whether or not to list self-defeating personality disorder along with the other official personality disorders in *DSM-IV* (APA 1994). The decision was made not to include this diagnosis.

It is not within the scope of this book to address the various issues and debates over potential misapplications of this diagnosis (i.e., to what extent is the construct of masochism gender-biased as opposed to the sociocultural factors that foster masochism). Rather, masochism is viewed as a personality disorder that is commonly presented by both sexes, especially when considered as a component of a mixed personality disorder, which best represents most patients seen by the authors. As Blum (1977) notes,

> There is no evidence that the human female has a greater endowment to derive pleasure from pain or a lesser capacity for neutralization and secondary autonomy ... Masochism is neither essentially feminine nor a valuable component of mature female function and character. [pp. 187–188]

Furthermore, as Meyers (1988) notes, early developmental issues of narcissistic compensations for love, separation, self-delineation, and lost omnipotence represent masochistic functions in both sexes.

> Any greater frequency of masochism in women, as evidenced by masochistic sexual fantasies and general masochistic behavior, has been attributed to other factors relating to early development, child rearing, and socialization, such as: ego ideal factors involving identification with a mother's masochistic self-representation; parental attitudes toward boys and girls; and the realities of greater male power and privilege in our culture—all these leading to seduction of the aggressor; masochism being the "weapon of the weak." [p. 186]

As lack of relatedness may still be more acceptable to the male gender role than submission is (and vice versa for the female gender role) more women may have problems with painful overattachment while more men may have problems with painful underattachment.

Finally, the authors believe that eliminating the term *masochism* does not eliminate the problem, because the masochistic or self-defeating personality is a common personality disorder in the population (APA, 1987). This observation is supported by the proliferation of popular psychology literature that addresses masochistic issues (Forward 1986, Norwood 1985). Included among these are books on co-dependency (Beattie 1987) and adult children of alcoholics (Woititz 1983). Furthermore, self-help groups for co-dependency and adult children of alcoholics seem to have emerged everywhere. Characteristics of co-dependents include (a) exaggerated caretaking, (b) difficulty receiving (including compliments and praise), (c) propensity for self-blame, (d) feeling unloved unless needed, (e) use of denial, (f) difficulty with loss, (g) difficulty setting limits, (h) equating love and pain, (i) remaining in difficult relationships, (j) problems in trusting one's perceptions, and (k) difficulty expressing anger (Beattie 1987). All of these characteristics are common components of the masochistic personality disorder.

Whether the term *masochistic* is changed to *self-defeating, co-dependent,* or another label entirely, it is the responsibility of mental health professionals to respond to this outcry to help the numerous patients who suffer from this problem. While self-help groups may provide masochists with a nondestructive selfobject experience, they are not able to help them to complete the separation-individuation process. Thus, psychotherapy remains an important method for treatment.

Despite the controversy surrounding the term *masochism,* we believe that it denotes a rich and instructive conceptualization and warrants clarifying efforts aimed at helping clinicians refine their diagnosis and understanding of this disorder in order to provide better treatment to the many patients struggling with masochistic issues. The purpose of this book is to facilitate an understanding of the evolving definitions of masochism, describe masochism at the preneurotic level, and discuss the etiological origins of this disorder and its multiple functions. A general approach to object relations therapy is described and applied to the masochistic personality, in particular. In this approach, the therapist attempts to modify the patient's internal and external object relations by providing him or her with a corrective interpersonal experience. Clinicians are helped to understand how they can differentiate masochistic personalities from patients with related disorders, and the typical countertransference problems that therapists encounter in treating masochistic patients will be discussed. Finally, couples and group approaches to treatment will be described.

2

Current
Conceptualizations
of Masochism

HISTORICAL ROOTS OF MASOCHISM

The following synopsis cites some of the more salient understandings and transformations related to the construct of masochism as well as the basic formulations ascribed to by the current authors. The psychological concept of masochism was originally introduced by Krafft-Ebing (1895), who employed the term to designate a sexual perversion in which erotic pleasure was derived from the passive-submission to or the active seeking out of cruel and/or humiliating behaviors rendered by a beloved other. Krafft-Ebing believed that cultivated or noncongenital masochism developed from the persistent pairing of lust for a significant other with the idea of being tyrannized so that eventually the lustful emotion transferred to the tyranny itself and resulted in variations of "sexual bondage."

Berliner (1958) noted that Krafft-Ebing's sexual masochists were consistently depicted as love hungry children "sensually in love" with a parent figure who "was cruel and punishing but also sexually complying" (p. 40). Being attracted to someone who *both* punishes *and* gratifies has thus been an integral component of the psychic conceptualization of masochism from its point of origination.

In his seminal writings on masochism, Freud (1905, 1919, 1924) highlighted and expanded on Krafft-Ebing's theorizing, underscoring not the masochistic "pleasure in pain and cruelty" but "the pleasure secured in all kinds of humiliation and submission" (1924, p. 169). Freud (1924) proposed that any intense stimulation, including psychic distress and painful physical tensions, could arouse sexual excitement during infancy. This mechanism supposedly provided the physiological basis for erotogenic or sexual masochism ("the lust of pain," p. 159), which Freud considered the substrate of all other masochistic formulations. This idea has persisted with Bieber (1966) noting that anxiety may similarly stimulate and sustain such erotic excitement.

Freud (1924) also discriminated between sexual masochism ("the lust for pain"), feminine masochism (particularly in men, the desire to be treated as a helpless, dependent, but naughty child), and moral masochism, which he designated the "most important form in which masochism appears" (p. 157). Freud defined this latter form of masochism as "a norm of behavior" (p. 162) (as opposed to a sexual perversion) such that "it is the suffering itself that matters." Unlike sexual or feminine masochism, in moral masochism the deliverer no longer needs to be the love object but can be as impersonal as the forces of fate. What is important is that "the true masochist always holds out his cheek wherever he sees a chance of receiving a blow" (p. 170).

Freud proposed two theories to explain masochism.

The first, and most influential theory, viewed the essential masochistic process as the subject's own sadism toward a loved and hated object turned back on the self. The turning around of this instinct included a transformation of the original active aim to an attitude of passivity toward the ambivalently experienced parental authority/love object. Ultimately the subject would seek still another person who would assume the subject's original sadistic role and thus satisfy the subject's unconscious feeling of guilt.

Freud's (1924) second theory, which was subsequently criticized and then dropped by post-Freudian writers, viewed masochism as an expression of the death instinct (primary masochism), the aim being the gratification of an unconscious feeling of guilt about forbidden impulses, which translated into "a need for punishment by an authority figure" (p. 166). Freud believed masochists resolved this conflict by "resexualizing morality," thus setting up "a temptation to sinful acts which must then be expiated by the reproaches of the sadistic conscience . . . by chastisement from the great parental authority of Fate" (p. 169). Finally, Freud noted that moral masochism really evidenced "instinctual fusion" since the self-destructive urges originating in the death instinct had "the value of an erotic component" (p. 171) and thus resulted in a degree of libidinal gratification.

POST-FREUDIAN THEORIES OF MASOCHISM

Reich (1933) and Bieber (1966) have emphasized that the evidence indicates that masochists do not take pleasure in pain per se, but are resigned to endure suffering as a necessary prerequisite to get what they need and/or enjoy. Reich proposed that masochism involved the choosing of the lesser injury such that one accepted a degree of punishment for forbidden sexual wishes, which saved one from the greater punishment of castration. The masochist's pleasure was thus due to the relief that castration was avoided. Reich believed further that masochistic characters, genetically hypersensitive to the psychic tension states of frustration or hurt, suffered deep childhood disappointments as the victims of aggression, and developed excessive needs for love. This love would be received, earned, or coerced through suffering at the hands of the love object. Reich emphasized both the coercive nature of masochists' suffering and the indirect expression of their aggression.

Horney (1939), whose views were more cultural and interpersonal, believed that masochistic suffering was an attempt to defend against injured omnipotence and deep feelings of insignificance or intrinsic weakness. Horney believed that "abandoning oneself to excessive suffering may serve as an opiate against pain" (p. 265) and the turning of passive victimization into active embracement of pain may enhance the masochist's sense of control. "Horney was anticipating later concepts of narcissistic vulnerability, injury, and the vicissitudes of infantile omnipotence as crucial factors in masochism" (Glick and Meyers 1988, p. 9).

Reik (1941) believed masochists sought the same pleasure that we all do as well as seeking to avoid the anxiety associated with anticipating punishment by voluntarily submitting to suffering. In so doing, masochists gain the right to enjoy previously denied gratifications, thus achieving victory in defeat. In like fashion, Horney (1939) also believed masochistic suffering was a way of relinquishing the self in order to avoid anxiety.

In contrast to Freud and Reik, Berliner (1947, 1958) stressed that masochism reflected an underlying ego disorder and object relations disturbance rather than an instinctual phenomenon and basically represented the turning of the love object's sadism (rather than one's own) upon oneself through the processes of introjection, identification, and superego formation. Berliner believed the critical element of masochism rested not on the masochist's projection of sadism and aggression but on the introjection of the object's sadism into the masochist's superego.

Berliner (1958) defined masochism as both a neurotic solution to the childhood conflict of loving a vitally needed other who gave nonlove (i.e., neglect, punishment, or guilt inducement) in return and a defensive reaction of the ego designed to protect the individual from a sense of total powerlessness. More specifically, masochism was viewed as the pre-oedipal child's attempt to get skin contact and love needs met with a nonloving or painful parent figure. Berliner, like Bergler (1961), thus underscored the connection between masochism and narcissistic injury, and he postulated that masochism was a defensive response to chronic empathic failures to the child's developing self, excessive parental ambivalence, and projections of hostility. Such theorizing anticipated authors like Kohut (1971, 1977), who wrote extensively on narcissism; Stolorow (1975) and Gear and Liendo (1981), who focused on the narcissistic function in masochism; and Cooper (1988), who described the narcissistic-masochistic character.

Gear and Liendo (1981) emphasized the "security ego" of the masochist, noting that masochists exchange unpleasure for security. While the "well organized, reality ego would accommodate both self-preservation and pleasure," the masochist seems compulsively to frustrate "himself by satisfying the other," but describes and perceives "himself as satisfied by frustrating the other" (pp. 228–230).

As Bernstein (1957) noted, the earlier efforts at explicating masochism focused on its libidinal aspects, while later efforts emphasized the defensive functions and the motivated attempts to maintain object relations. Brennan (1952) was the first author on masochism to integrate concepts from all three perspectives of id, superego, and ego psychology, noting that masochism was a complex constellation that incorporated components of each. As Stolorow (1975) would later point out: "masochistic manifestations . . . are multiply determined and serve multiple functions" at times including, "the narcissistic function of restoring and maintaining the structural cohesiveness, temporal stability and positive affective coloring of a precarious or crumbling self-representation" (p. 441).

From a self psychology perspective Stolorow (1975) recommended Rapaport's (1951) concept of the motivational hierarchy with masochism serving the superego and narcissism assuming lower priority in the neurotic individual with a relatively intact ego. For the structurally deficient individual with a "fragile self-representation, the narcissistic function will occupy a position of very high priority" (p. 441).

The masochistic personality described in this book represents a character organization that is primarily fixated at the level of separation-individuation where good self and object representations are differentiated but bad self and object representations are not. Individuals fixated at this stage of object relations most fear the loss of the significant other's love and approval and object loss as opposed to annihilation of the self. The authors also posit that masochism neither signifies a primarily sexual phenomenon nor the deriving of pleasure from pain but rather a pathological way of loving and individuating that reflects a disturbance in object relations and ego development.

For the current authors, a pathological way of loving includes (a) loving someone who predominantly or substantially gives nonlove in return (Berliner 1958), and who lends him- or herself to a relationship characterized in part by idealized symbiosis; (b) associating self-negation or submission and suffering with loving (e.g., "I need to subject my will to others to be loved," "I need to earn love through suffering"); (c) protecting the idealized image of an ambivalently experienced love object by introjecting, rationalizing, and/or denying the other's sadism; and finally (d) attempting to master the original conflict through repetition-compulsion by choosing critical and rejecting but admired love objects and attempting to win them over through pleasing and self-sacrifice.

It is important to note that what the masochist seeks is not the mature love of a healthy adult-to-adult relationship or the joys of loving the true self of the other. What masochists search for is what Nydes (1963) calls pre-oedipal or dependent love. "It is love which affirms weakness and the need for tender care and protection. It is as if the identity of the masochist is surrendered to the object whose power must then be employed in behalf of the weak one" (p. 56). Masochists thus seek to be nurtured, gratified, and emotionally held as a parent would a child. To earn this "protective custody," masochists appear to renounce their power to the other and then, in essence, take the other hostage by making the other responsible for the masochist's sense of well-being (i.e., internal security and self-esteem).

Furthermore, the authors define the masochistic way of individuating as referring to a process of projecting and/or anticipating the forceful domination of another's will and then resisting such domination via such tactics as (a) passive-aggressiveness or stubborn willfulness couched in a "yes-but" sense of semi-compliance, (b) assuming a caretaking role or an overcontrolled presentation that establishes a position of passive dominance, and (c) subtly provoking others into power struggles and/or acting out the masochist's own ambivalence and anger so as to give "justification" to the patient's need to differentiate and self-affirm through resistance or saying "no."

In the remaining chapters of this book, the authors will further elaborate on masochistic object relations and individuation as related to clinical description, structural issues, etiology, treatment goals and strategies, and differential diagnosis from hysteroid-borderline, narcissistic, obsessive-compulsive, and hysterical personality disorder.

3

Descriptive Clinical Overview

A woman working in her garden found a beautiful, wounded snake and brought it into her home in order to heal it. For months, she painstakingly nursed it back to health. When it was finally healed, the woman, admiring the snake's beauty, reached down to stroke it and the snake bit her. Surprised, the woman said to the snake, "Why did you bite me when I brought you into my home and cared for and healed you?" The snake replied, "But you knew that I was a snake when you brought me into your house."

The fable about the woman and the snake characterizes an essential element of the masochistic style. At the heart of this style lies a relational process whereby an individual tends to be attracted to caring for wounded souls, only to be confronted with a predominance of hate, hostile withdrawal, or selfish preoccupation. To continue with the analogy of the woman and the snake, a woman with a masochistic object relations template would tend to internalize the snake's view of the world and blame herself for the snake's hostile behavior. In addition, she would tend to idealize the snake, focusing on how beautiful the snake is and how it had wonderful potential if only she could "do or be the right thing." As a result of this internal process, she might encourage the snake to remain in her home while doing all she could to please the snake so that it would want to stay and not bite her again. In this analogy, the woman may eventually be left by this snake, yearn for the relationship and then bring home a second wounded snake, only to have the same scenario repeated.

Understanding patients who, like the woman with the snake, continue to engage in self-defeating relationships has long remained a challenging clinical puzzle. In this chapter we describe the behavior patterns that are the hallmark of the masochistic character. These patterns include (a) a relationship orientation, (b) problems in basic trust, (c) overdetermined caretaking, (d) difficulty receiving from others, (e) compliance-defiance conflicts, (f) problems with loss and separation, (g) internalizing relational difficulties, and (h) narcissistic issues.

RELATIONSHIP ORIENTATION

Most character styles have a dominant underlying motivation. Narcissists want admiration to shore up their fragile sense of self-esteem. Thus, much of their behavior is geared toward seeking admiration from others. Obsessive-impulsives try to gain a measure of existential security through the illusion of control and the feeling of being right (Wells et al. 1990). This leads them to participate in frequent arguments and power struggles. The paranoid personality seeks power as a means of self-protection (Nydes 1963). Relationships with others for them are thus fraught with themes of dominance and submission.

In contrast, a primary motive of the masochistic personality is the desire to love and be loved. As masochists are frequently very relationship oriented or other directed, they tend to spend a great deal of time around people, either caring for them or soliciting their love and approval. The masochist's life is often centered around relational opportunities. One masochistic patient said that she "had more friends than time." Another masochistic patient discussed her concern about missing any phone calls. She reported answering the phone both in the middle of the night and during sex with her partner (the telephone was kept beside her bed). She also had call-waiting service, so that her phone calls were interrupted when a second person called. This patient didn't want to miss any phone calls as, for reasons that will be described in Chapter 4, happiness for the masochist involves never being alone. However, unlike borderline patients, they are ambivalent about dependency and thus tend to become attached to more than one person.

PROBLEMS WITH BASIC TRUST

One reason that masochists often develop such large relationship systems is that they fundamentally don't trust people to be reliable and predictable. One solution to needing others, while not trusting them, is to "not put all your eggs in one basket." One masochistic patient said that she "always kept her refrigerator full so that she'd never be hungry."

Masochists have difficulty trusting people because of

their past and current experiences of being abused by others. Like the woman and the snake, masochists are often attracted to wounded souls that "bite them" (i.e., become critical, rejecting, and selfish). One masochistic patient left her husband for a man who began to reject her as soon as she became available. A male patient chose a woman who, like his mother, constantly berated him.

By reenacting childhood experiences of scapegoating and abuse, masochists tend to solidify an internal mental representation of themselves as a victim. One patient, for example, saw herself as fated to be involved with critical, selfish men who would abandon her for other women. Her father behaved that way toward her mother, with whom she was identified. Another patient constantly found herself in jobs where her employees were irritated at her, like her father was, for not complying with their "rigid rules."

The masochist's sense of victimization, however, has a paradoxical quality. While masochists don't trust others and expect to be hurt, they often blame themselves for relational difficulties. For example, one patient expressed that if she were not so "neurotic and depressed all the time, her husband wouldn't seek comfort from other women." Another patient said that if only she "had kept the dog in the yard [as he requested], her husband would not have kicked him." Due to internal conflicts and defenses described later in this chapter, masochists struggle with the need for and fear of the object and some confusion about where the source of relational difficulties lies.

DIFFICULTY RECEIVING FROM OTHERS

Thus, while masochists have a great wish for caring relationships with people, because of their fear of being hurt and disappointed they have difficulty receiving love and help from others. Caretaking from others is regarded with suspicion and mistrust as though it were a "Trojan horse" (Glickauf-Hughes and Wells 1991). For example, one patient recalled an experience as a child in which his teacher stroked his hair. Just as he was allowing himself to experience pleasure at receiving affection, his teacher "whacked him on the back of the head." He thus remains extremely ambivalent about asking for and receiving affection from others. While he desperately desires love and affection, he fears that if he gets it, it will "turn bad."

In addition to having difficulty receiving love and affection, masochists have difficulty accepting compliments. Panken (1983) noted that masochists "cannot stand praise." As masochists often "act nice" when they feel critical and angry, they assume that other people are also insincere in their praise.

The authors have observed a common pattern in families of masochists in which one parent was experienced as critical and the other parent was experienced as a Pollyanna or salesperson type. As masochists suspected that the complimentary parent had an underlying negative regard for them, they viewed that parent as inauthentic and saw the critical parent as more honest. For example, one patient reported that when he was an adult, his father (who was a coach) informed him that he had given him so many pep talks as a child to build up his confidence (not because the father genuinely valued him). Another patient stated that "all mothers think their daughters are pretty."

Masochists tend to experience compliments as "phony" and as masking an underlying devaluation of them. Transferring anticipated hypocrisy unto others, they vigilantly discount positive (but potentially insincere) expressions so that they will never be "tricked" by believing insincere compliments again. Thus, one patient thought that her boyfriend only told her that she was beautiful in order "to make her feel good because he knew that she was so insecure." Another patient said that his boss gave him a glowing work evaluation because the "boss was a nice guy and gave everyone good evaluations."

Masochistic patients also tend to discount anything positive from the therapist. One patient stated that while the therapist seemed to regard her positively and treated her well, "it was her job to act that way." Another patient said that while the therapist seemed to like him, it was only because the therapist was such a caring person.

OVERDETERMINED CARETAKING

One solution to the masochist's need-fear dilemma is to gain interpersonal control by assuming the dominant nurturing role in relationships. Masochists quite often tend to be caretakers (Gear et al. 1981) who treat others as they wish to be treated themselves. For example, one patient frequently showered his wife with affection even though she sometimes found this intrusive. Assuming the caretaker role in relationships thus allows masochists to get their own dependency needs met vicariously without being vulnerable (and thus potentially victimized) themselves.

Another reason for overdetermined caretaking is that masochists believe that they are loved for what they do for others, not for who they are. Masochists thus often behave altruistically as a means of gaining love and approval. They unconsciously give to others as a means of earning being given to in return. For example, one patient constantly filled in for colleagues who were sick, hoping that they would like and appreciate him. Their giving thus subtly puts others in their debt. This accounts, in part, for other people becoming annoyed with them when they are trying to be helpful. This is particularly the case when they choose narcissistic partners (who don't want to be in anyone's debt).

Masochists' solicitous behavior thus often provides an indirect clue to loved ones about what they want or need themselves. Due to their discomfort with their own needs and mistrust of others, masochists tend to be unaware of what they need from people and ashamed to ask that their needs be gratified when they do know what they want. Thus, one patient tended to shower his wife with kisses when he really needed affection himself (but either wasn't aware of this need or was afraid to ask that it be met directly).

In addition to providing relational control, vicarious need gratification, and clues or justification for being given to, caretaking provides masochists with a sense of identity and increases their self-esteem. It is common to find masochistic patients who are in the helping professions. Furthermore, they are often married to (and responsible for) people who are unemployed, alcoholic, or otherwise in trouble. They also tend to receive frequent calls from needy friends who they comfort and care for.

COMPLIANCE-DEFIANCE CONFLICT

In addition to overdetermined caretaking, the masochist's relational need-fear dilemma is manifested through help-rejecting, complaining behaviors. While masochists frequently complain and solicit the advice and help of others, when help is offered they tend to reject it. Thus, when therapists respond to masochistic patients' requests for advice, they often encounter a profusion of reasons why the advice won't work. For example, one patient frequently complained about being injured or intruded upon by her psychotic mother (who wouldn't take her medication). She wouldn't hospitalize her mother, however, when the therapist suggested it, because she said that she felt too guilty. Another patient asked her friends to help her decorate her new house. When they came over to help her, she didn't like any of their suggestions.

While masochistic patients consciously want help (or a reunion with a loving mother), an unconscious aim is to gain a sense of control over a cruel and damaging mother (Cooper and Fischer 1981). Thus, in the previous example (of the masochistic patient who wouldn't hospitalize her psychotic mother), when her mother came to visit, she stayed busy working. She eventually hospitalized her, feeling exasperated and angry.

What this example demonstrates is that masochists have a great deal of suppressed, ego-dystonic anger that is usually expressed indirectly. So much pressure has been put on them to "act nice and be good" that they tend to behave in an overtly pleasing, solicitous, self-effacing manner. However, due to a history of being abused and over-controlled, they often feel willful, ambivalent, and angry (Johnson 1985). The latter behaviors are commonly expressed through passive provocation and whining. For example, one patient (who was angry at her husband) made a special trip to the store to buy him cereal and bought him the wrong kind of cereal. She couldn't understand why he was frustrated with her when she had been so considerate. Another patient (whose wife forgot his birthday) didn't mention this omission but complained all night (in a whiny voice) about his boss. As these patients are often unaware of their feelings (and expressions) of stubbornness or anger, they are frequently surprised by other people's hostile reactions to them when they are trying so desperately to "be nice and to get along with people."

PROBLEMS WITH LOSS AND SEPARATION

A common complaint of masochistic patients that elicits massive "yes-but" behavior in the face of advice is chronic, abusive relationships. One reason that masochists have such great difficulty leaving relationships that seem to cause them significant pain is that one of their primary conflict areas is loss and separation (Avery 1977). When faced with interpersonal difficulties with the significant others in their lives, masochists will sacrifice their good feelings (including their good opinion of themselves) before giving up their love object. Thus, many a battered wife fearing loss explains that her husband hit her because she provoked him, that she knew he was having a bad day and she should have been more sensitive to him.

The thought of leaving their partner is so terrifying to masochists that they tend to distort their perception of the object through denial and rationalization rather than to leave the partner. Masochists believe that if they left their partner, the enormous emotional pain and regression that they would experience would completely overwhelm their egos. They believe that the pain that they would face if they separated from their partner would be exponentially greater than any pain that they endure in the relationship. Relational pain for masochists is the lesser of the two evils, the greater evil being separation anxiety. As will be further described in Chapter 4, masochistic patients' difficulty with loss and separation is related in part to their incomplete sense of object constancy.

USE OF INTERNALIZATION

As preserving the relationship with the significant other (and avoiding separation anxiety) is the masochist's primary goal, masochists tend to use defense mechanisms to help them accomplish this goal. In addition to denying and rationalizing the object's sadistic or aggressive behavior, the masochist has a strong propensity to internalize interpersonal problems. Thus, when experiencing conflicts with the significant others in their lives, masochists tend to blame themselves for the relational difficulty. They believe that if their partner is angry at them, they must in some way be bad or defective. For example, one patient reported that her husband was angry at her because the cat's litter box wasn't clean. He responded by throwing the cat against the wall. This patient expressed a great sense of guilt and remorse for provoking his behavior by failing to clean the litter box. It was less painful for her to view herself as a "bad," inconsiderate wife than to see her husband as a "bad," sadistic husband whom she might have to leave.

In addition to avoiding potential separations, masochists tend to internalize relational problems (i.e., self-blame) as a means of gaining a sense of control over their "bad fate" (Glickauf-Hughes and Wells 1991). Given that masochists assume that they will inevitably be hurt, punished, and criticized by their partner, they prefer that the blame be self-inflicted in order to get a greater sense of control over the pain. For example, one masochistic patient criticized her body on a daily basis as a means of preventing herself from getting fat and thus inducing criticism from her narcissistic partner.

Masochists also tend to internalize relational problems due to a propensity to use the defense mechanism referred to by Meyers (1988) as masochistic splitting.

Masochists tend to perceive others as whole objects and thus infrequently view the object as "all bad." However, they tend to lack integration within their self-structure and thus have the propensity not only to blame themselves but to experience themselves as "all bad" at times. For example, one masochistic patient reported that his wife told him that she didn't do what he requested because he was so controlling. He responded by feeling not only like a controlling person but like "a terrible husband and a bad human being who no one could love." The pattern of masochistic splitting will be described in greater detail in Chapter 4. For now, what is important to understand is that the process of internalizing relational problems to avoid separating from the needed, sadistic object is intensified by experiencing the self as "all bad."

NARCISSISTIC ISSUES

A connection has been noted in the literature between narcissism and masochism. Stolorow (1975) has observed how masochistic behavior can have narcissistic functions. Cooper (1988) discusses how these traits are often integrated in the same character. The literature has noted a predominance of narcissistic traits in masochists (Glickauf-Hughes and Wells 1991). Clinically, the authors have observed a number of masochistic patients who seem to struggle with narcissistic issues. These include (a) self-esteem regulation, (b) perfectionism, (c) audience sensitivity, (d) the imposter phenomenon, and (e) the regressive role in a narcissistic collusion.

Self-Esteem Regulation

While masochists have a reasonably consolidated and differentiated sense of self, they frequently have difficulty maintaining a sense of self-esteem. In addition to feeling bad or defective and blaming themselves for relational problems, masochists have difficulty appreciating their own virtues and forgiving themselves for their mistakes. For example, one extremely competent, attractive, and successful masochistic patient constantly berated herself for being stupid and ugly and felt in constant fear of losing her job and being left by her husband for someone more beautiful. Another patient, although charming and personable, had difficulty believing that anyone would really like and want to be friends with him. The structural components of this problem will be discussed in greater detail in Chapter 4.

Perfectionism

One reason for the masochists' low self-esteem is their unrealistically high ego ideal. Masochists expect perfection of themselves in the areas that they deem to be important (e.g., beauty, intelligence). One particular quality that most masochists aspire to is "perfect goodness." They believe that they should always be fair, patient, and generous, and are critical of themselves when they are not. For example, one patient, who was a therapist herself, was very self-critical when she didn't feel empathy toward her patients. Masochists often have an unrealistic image of what constitutes a "good enough" human being. This view is constantly reinforced by the objects in their lives.

However, while masochists strive for perfection (especially perfect goodness) their motives for achieving perfection are different from narcissistic patients. Masochists wish to be perfect to gain love and avoid rejection. They believe that they will not be loved and accepted for being their true selves, and fear that minor transgressions will lead to their being abandoned. This belief is reinforced by the masochist's propensity to select narcissistic and borderline individuals as partners who indeed behave this way toward them (Glickauf-Hughes 1994, Glickauf-Hughes and Wells 1991).

Audience Sensitivity

As a means of avoiding displeasing others (and thus becoming abandoned), masochists have learned to be highly attuned to what others (particularly loved ones) want and need. One patient expressed that when her husband sat down in front of the television with a beer and a particular expression on his face, she could tell that he was feeling bad and needing comfort.

Masochists have also learned to be highly attuned to danger signals from other people (although they tend at times to deny them). One patient talked about how when his wife came home and had a particular tone of voice, he knew that if he was not careful with her she would become angry and abusive with him. While many people are sensitive to their partner's needs and feelings, masochists are vigilant about this and believe that maintaining a loving relationship is contingent upon their excelling at this function. This skill is one reason that people with masochistic character structures often make excellent psychotherapists. Masochists thus work very hard to earn love and affection.

Imposter Phenomenon (Clance and Imes 1978)

Due to feeling conditionally loved (only if they're good and perfect) and feeling an inner sense of low self-worth, masochists often feel like impostors in the world. They believe that they can only be loved for being their kind, altruistic, false self, and that if people only knew how angry and selfish they really were, they would be rejected.

Thus, while one masochistic patient was a popular high school teacher and had a veritable village of friends, he believed that they liked and admired his false-self behavior—not him. Another patient believed that if she did not work 150 percent at things, she would fail. This pattern is related to and exacerbated by the masochist's tendency to discounted compliments. Compliments from others are perceived as being ungenuine. Not believing compliments reinforces the masochist's low self-esteem.

Regressive Narcissism (Willi 1982)

In a narcissistic collusion, masochists tend to take the regressive narcissistic position or the admiring role (Glick-auf-Hughes 1994). Thus, masochists attempt to repair their fragile sense of self-esteem by choosing an idealized partner and identifying with him or her. Masochists thus have a propensity to make narcissistic object choices. One masochistic patient (who felt unattractive) would only date handsome men. Another patient (who felt insecure about her ability to accomplish her own career goals) only became involved with extremely successful men. Both patients believed that by being associated with partners they idealized in a way that they felt defective themselves, the partner's beauty and success would somehow "rub off" onto them. The woman in the fable was attracted to the snake because of its beauty (as well as its danger).

In conclusion, to return to the original fable of the woman and the snake, the following hypotheses may be drawn about the woman's motivations. The woman was accustomed to being around snakes who told her that they weren't snakes. She was thus in the habit of denying their predilection to bite people. She was intrigued by the snake's beauty and was accustomed to caring for beautiful, wounded (but unpredictable) creatures. There was a great challenge in being a "snake charmer." Finally, when the snake bit her, she blamed herself for mishandling the snake as she had become attached to him and very much wished to keep him as her pet. She hoped that if she could learn to handle him better, he would learn not to bite. It was difficult for her to acknowledge that biting was in the snake's nature.

The major features that contribute to individuals selecting and remaining in difficult relationships have been described. We now turn to the structural dynamics of these traits in Chapter 4, followed by their developmental and interpersonal origins in Chapter 5.

4

Preneurotic
Masochism

The masochistic character disorder described in the previous chapter is conceptualized as being structured at the preneurotic level of ego/object relations development (Horner 1979, Varga 1985). Preneurotic ego structure represents a level of ego/object relations development more advanced than Kernberg's (1975) borderline ego organization and less advanced than Kernberg's neurotic ego organization. Horner first coined the term *preneurotic* and proposed that it refer to a character pathology that remains arrested at the stage of development at which, according to Mahler and colleagues (1975), the child is on the way to object constancy (22 to 30 months), a period covering the latter phase of rapprochement and the beginning of the fourth stage of separation-individuation. On the way to object constancy is the period of development where the child solidifies identity and autonomy, and via transmuting internalizations of maternal functions "achieves

O. Stern

an internalized source of comfort and love. With this internalization, the other is seen more and more as a person in his or her own right rather than as a narcissistically cathected part of the child's self" (Johnson 1987, p. 33).

In addition, this internalization process helps the child move from fear of object loss to fear of the loss of the object's love and approval. As Horner (1979, p. 36) originally noted, preneurotic individuals have failed to complete "the final shift to object constancy and a well-secured separate identity, with the capacity to regulate one's narcissistic equilibrium from the sources within the self."

The preneurotic's failure to complete the assimilation of maternal functions (such as soothing and realistically based self-regard) into self-representation leaves the individual susceptible to depression and overly dependent upon a somewhat idealized other in order to stabilize his or her internal security and self-esteem. Because the preneurotic ego–object relations organization has not been described in any detail in the psychoanalytic literature, this chapter (a) briefly chronicles the evolutionary context in which the authors propose the preneurotic level of masochistic character development; (b) describes in some detail the specific structural and defensive hallmarks of preneurotic masochism, including the strong propensity for masochistic splitting and anxious attachment; and (c) explicitly differentiates neurotic, preneurotic, and borderline masochism. Chapter 5 discusses in detail the various factors involved in the etiology of preneurotic masochism.

EVOLVING STRUCTURAL/DEVELOPMENTAL CONTEXTS

There has been much speculation in the psychoanalytic literature as to the developmental stage in which the masochistic personality is formed. For example, Reich (1933), like Freud (1924), saw masochism as an oedipal-level phenomenon. Johnson (1985) understood the masochistic personality as developing during the later anal/separation-individuation stage of ego development. In contrast, it has been postulated that masochism originates at the oral stage (Panken 1983) or the symbiotic level of ego development (Menaker 1953).

In addition to disputes over the developmental stage of origination, various authors have also disagreed upon the functional uses of masochism. For example, the earlier efforts at explicating masochism (e.g., Freud 1924, Reich 1933) focused on its libidinal aspects while later efforts have emphasized its defensive functions and the unconsciously motivated attempts to maintain object relations (Bernstein 1957).

Many recent authors (e.g., Bergler 1961, Glick and Meyers 1988, Mollinger 1982, Stolorow 1975) have suggested that masochism can be structured at more than one level of ego/object relations development. Bergler (1961) observed two types of masochism: neurotic and malignant, representing oedipal versus pre-oedipal developmental arrests. As a result of similar observations, Mollinger (1982) postulated that masochism could best be understood in terms of fixations or regressions to any of three developmental stages (symbiotic, separation-individuation, oedipal) and that the character structures formed in each stage were different. Arrests at the symbiotic stage produced sadomasochistic individuals who feared annihilation and loss of self. Arrests at the separation-individuation stage were marked by masochistic individuals who feared loss of object love, while arrests at the oedipal stage produced individuals who felt guilty over forbidden impulses.

Stolorow (1975) recommended Rapaport's (1951) concept of the motivational hierarchy with "the relative dominance of a particular meaning or function of masochistic symptomatology [varying] from patient to patient" (Meyers 1988, p. 175), depending upon the level at which the character pathology is structured. Differentially diagnosing masochism structured at various developmental stages becomes important in anticipating and understanding transference and countertransference issues as well as salient treatment considerations.

Similarly to Mollinger (1982), we propose that masochism can be structured at three different levels of ego and object relations development and that masochism serves different functions at different levels of structuralization. These three levels of structuralization are (a) the neurotic or oedipal stage of ego and object relations organization, (b) the preneurotic or advanced separation-individuation stage (i.e., on the way to object constancy), and (c) the borderline or earlier separation-individuation phases (e.g., rapprochement, practicing) of ego and object relations organization.

NEUROTIC, BORDERLINE, AND PRENEUROTIC MASOCHISM

In general, masochism manifests more depressive perfectionism, guilt, and shame at more advanced levels of structuralization (neurotic and preneurotic), while demonstrating more impulsivity at the borderline level where a substantial sadistic component interpenetrates the character pathology (Kernberg 1988). As masochism becomes more primitively structured (e.g., borderline), depressive perfectionism and guilt are replaced by primitive sexualization of needs and severe self-destructiveness, such as self-mutilation and impulsive suicidal gestures (Kernberg

1975). In addition, the more primitive the level of ego and object relations development, the more that masochism serves needed narcissistic functions as opposed to serving an overly harsh, but well-integrated superego (Stolorow 1975). Masochism structured at the preneurotic level of ego and object relations reflects a stable, enduring mixture of characteristics including the more oedipal-level symptoms of depressive perfectionism and excessive self-criticism as well as relatively mild pre-oedipal level deficits in self-soothing, self-activation, and self-integration.

PRENEUROTIC MASOCHISM

In contrast to borderline sadomasochism where self-cohesion is in great jeopardy, preneurotic masochists have achieved substantial ego cohesion, a stable sense of temporal continuity, and basically good reality testing and object relatedness. Their clinical presentation more closely resembles the symptomatology of the neurotic masochist, but at the preneurotic level masochistic behavior and traits serve structural aims such as self-soothing and basic security as opposed to satisfying demands for punishment by an overly harsh, oedipal superego.

According to Horner (1979), the preneurotic masochist's failure to complete "the final shift to object constancy and a well-secured identity" (p. 36) results from the preneurotic's intense ambivalence toward the mother figure and his or her consequent resistance to identifying with the mother's realistic functions or capabilities (e.g., soothing, self-regard, belonging, confidence in problem solving). As previously noted, this failure to complete the assimilation of maternal functions into the self-representation leaves the individual vulnerable to depression and overly dependent upon a somewhat idealized other in order to stabilize his or her internal security and self-esteem. While the designated idealized other is often a romantic partner, it can also manifest in relationship to a job or a career. There may be gender-specific tendencies such that women may be prone to act out their masochistic issues in relationships whereas men tend to act out their masochistic issues in relation to their work (Pestrak, personal communication, 1987).

While Horner (1979) and Johnson (1987) believe that preneurotic masochists manifest little grandiosity, we have observed a predictable secret grandiosity in many preneurotic masochists. Such grandiosity serves as an often unconscious compensatory defense against their more conscious feelings of inferiority and worthlessness. This secret grandiosity is often revealed through attitudes that reflect a Miss Goody Two-Shoes type or exaggerated feelings of superiority supported by unnecessary and excessive self-sacrifice.

STRUCTURAL HALLMARKS OF PRENEUROTIC MASOCHISM

Incomplete transmuting internalizations of realistic maternal functions are related to structural issues such as identity formation or self-definition (e.g., "I am a sufferer," "I am never good enough"); self-esteem ("I'm worthy when I suffer," "I am secure through my attachment to a designated idealized other"); object attachment ("I must submit my will to the other to maintain a relationship"); anxious attachment; and strivings for individuation ("You can't stop me from being self-destructive when I want to be," "I make my own pain because I like it"). Masochistic attitudes and behaviors are designed to enable individuals to maintain their attachment to the parental ego ideal or critical internal object from whom they are unable to completely separate due to intense and unresolved ambivalence. This phenomenon is also one of the critical reasons why the irrational bond to the bad object is so difficult to break.

In terms of identity development, the preneurotic masochist manifests a relatively unexpressed, unacknowledged, or unknown real self rather than a noncohesive or unformed real self representation (Johnson 1987, p. 34). The achievement of a definite individuality has been compromised in part because of the preneurotic masochist's reactive identity formation (e.g., "I do not want to be like my mother," who often manifests narcissistic tendencies). Inasmuch as the preneurotic masochist develops an other-oriented reactive stance and a self-definition that revolves around pathological altruism, individuality (which requires proactive autonomous self development) will remain stunted.

DEFENSIVE HALLMARKS OF PRENEUROTIC MASOCHISM

While our clinical observations support Horner's basic conceptualizations, we differ with Horner's belief that preneurotics completely substitute intense ambivalence for the splitting defense. In contrast, we have observed that while the integration of core identity appears to be maintained in less intimate or less narcissistically invested areas of the individual's life, preneurotic masochists will sacrifice this integration through the use of "masochistic splitting" (e.g. Horner 1979, Meyers 1988) whenever they perceive that a primary security attachment is being seriously jeopardized.

Primary masochistic attachments are usually maintained at high cost, so that while the preneurotic masochist typically experiences intense ambivalence toward the security object, masochistic splitting can temporarily occur during transient and reversible regressions that can follow ego as well as psychosexual lines of development. One of the primary hallmarks of preneurotic masochists is that while they are able to function quite well in many areas of their lives and have a substantially differentiated and cohesive self, the integration of their good and bad self and object representations is repeatedly sacrificed to masochistic splitting when they sense that the designated security attachment is being seriously jeopardized or threatened, particularly by their strivings for autonomy. Masochistic splitting can take a number of forms, two of which are prototypical.

The first form of masochistic splitting described by Meyers (1988) is a more primitive (and thus more simplified) intrapsychic split in which "the bad is split off from the object image . . . which is maintained as all good while the self becomes all bad in a kind of 'identification with the aggressor.' Aggression and punishment is then directed against the bad self" (p. 181), thus gratifying aggression while protecting the goodness of the security object and avoiding retaliation.

This form of masochistic splitting thus allows masochists to avoid the threat of object loss or further rejection by redirecting their own anger against the needed object's hatefulness toward their self (Stolorow and Lachman 1980). The masochist's tendency toward justifying the object's abuse may be understood in terms of "internalization of and identification with the hostile caretakers of childhood" (Young and Gerson 1991, p. 34). Fairbairn

(1954) explained the child's psychological adaptation to the predominately hostile parent by

> the concept of taking upon himself the burden of badness which appears to reside in his objects. . . . The child would rather be bad himself than have bad objects . . . In becoming bad . . . he seeks to purge (his objects) of their badness . . . Outer security is thus purchased at the price of inner security. [p. 65]

The second form of masochistic splitting (Horner 1979) is more complicated and involves converting the internal conflict into an external one through triangulating with a third party. Masochistic triangulation is motivated by masochists' desire to avoid their own anger, hate, and resentment toward a needed security object in order to maintain their good self experience. This is accomplished by designating another person to hold the rage the masochist feels toward the disappointing object so that the good self will not become the bad object with whom the good self is still symbiotically tied.

As a result, Horner (1979) states that the masochistic response to experiences of suffering and pain at the hands of the designated security object (who at this point is the bad object or persecutor) is to seek out the support, comfort, and validation of a third party who now serves as the designated rescuer or good object. "Tapping into the archaic, unconscious anger of the child victim of the designated rescuing object the masochistic individual is often quite successful in mobilizing the listener's anger toward the bad object" (p. 176). The designated rescuer commonly urges the masochist to leave the obviously destructive relationship or actively supports the masochist's anger or self assertion with the destructive other without recognizing the importance of the bad object's security functions.

Horner (1979) notes that this interpersonal process serves several defensive functions. Once the masochist's anger has been "validated it is experienced as morally justified and can therefore be assimilated into the good self" (p. 176). The masochist thus "avoids having to face the depths of his or her own bad self anger with its destructive potential" (p. 176). In addition the masochist can also avoid the conflict inherent in the experience of intense ambivalence toward the object by inducing the designated rescuer to contain the masochist's hate for the bad object of the security relationship. Once this happens the bond between the masochist and the security object can then be "defended on the basis of its importance and the love that can now be felt for the object" (p. 177).

A brief example may demonstrate how this defensive style can be manifested. Catherine, a 40-year-old white female, struggled with feelings of depression and self-doubt in a fifteen-year marriage to a man who suffered from episodic alcohol abuse. When inebriated, he would become exquisitely sensitive, taking offense easily and then threatening to leave the marriage because she was so hard to live with saying that "no one wants to live with someone who's depressed all the time." She would react to these episodes with abandonment panic and by trying even harder to please him. She said that she would "stand on her head and spit nickels, but nothing seemed to work." Eventually, she would call a friend to get advice on what to do, describing her situation in self-denigrating terms, inspiring anger in her friends against her husband. They would say, "He's so mean to you, why do you stay with him?" Catherine would then end up defending her husband by recounting how he had been under a lot of stress at work and how she had been no fun lately. "He isn't always like this, you know. It's just that he's so stressed out. He might not even be like this if he was with someone who had more energy and was more fun." It is important to note that during these episodes, Catherine always remained functional at work and maintained her long-term friendships.

In addition to specialized splitting defenses, the preneurotic masochist also employs projective identifications of a characteristic nature. Like Ogden (1979), we subscribe to the position that clinicians can find clients of all levels of pathology using projective identifications. The primary distinction between more developmentally advanced projective identifications and those that reflect more primitive ego and object relations development has to do with the degree of distortion in the client's projection and the intensity of the induced feeling state.

Finally, anxious attachment, the sine qua non of masochistic behavior, is defined as persistent and urgent clinging to a preferred person without there being apparent conditions to account for it (Ainsworth et al. 1969). Individuals who exhibit anxious attachment have "no confidence that their attachment figures will be accessible and responsive to them when they want them to be" and these individuals have thus "adopted a strategy of remaining in close proximity to them in order so far as possible for them to be available" (Bowlby 1973, p. 213).

Anxious attachment is believed to be caused by experiences that shake an individual's confidence in the availability of attachment figures when they are needed (Bowlby 1973). While early loss and separations are often indicated as etiological factors, threats to abandon the child are thought to be the most influential precipitant (Fairbairn 1954).

We believe that anxious attachment behaviors in the adult preneurotic masochist can be explained to a great extent by the structural deficits that arise as a result of the masochist's early experiences of inconsistent, egocentric, and intermittently hostile or cruel parenting. These chronic early attachment experiences with needed primary objects have two effects on the preneurotic's identification processes. As discussed earlier, the first effect is that the masochist tends to internalize the parental view of the child's badness in order to maintain the illusion of some control, which emanates from the belief that if the masochist can only become a better person, love and security will follow (Fairbairn 1952).

The second effect was described by Horner (1979). The preneurotic masochist tends to experience intense, often unconscious, ambivalence toward the maternal figure. In an attempt to avoid becoming like the mother, the masochist resists completing identifications with the mother's realistic soothing capacities. The failure to identify with these capacities leaves the masochist vulnerable to self-esteem injuries, depression, and excessive dependence upon others for soothing functions. As a result of this vulnerability and dependency the masochist is especially afraid of object loss or lack of object availability. This fear is mitigated by anxious attachment behavior and by the use of denial or masochist splitting.

An example of this behavior is illustrated by Catherine's repeated requests for reassurance by her husband. Catherine's insecurity about her lovability led her to ask her husband on an almost daily basis to tell her if he thought she was fat. She would ask. He would answer. She would then say, "Are you sure?" Often he would then feel a little annoyed and snap back. Catherine would then use this reaction as evidence to affirm her unlovableness and feel depressed. She would also feel clingy and try harder to improve herself and regain her husband's favor. She would usually apologize for being silly and try to win him over through cooking something for him that she knew he loved.

Individuals with personality structures fixated at the preneurotic stage of object relations thus fear the loss of the significant other's love and approval as well as fearing object loss, abandonment, and consequently the loss of their basic sense of security. For preneurotic masochists, separation from the chosen security object remains immensely difficult for a number of reasons. Most importantly, the object attachment is serving to provide for the masochist what the masochist cannot readily provide for the self due to (a) structural deficits at the stage of "on the way to object constancy" and (b) entrenched defenses that deny aspects of the real self and thus much vitality or passion for living.

It may also be noted that the individuals at the preneurotic level of structural development typically enter therapy with some of their self-defeating traits, defenses, and behavior described as ego-dystonic or problematic while other symptomatology remains ego-syntonic and is not seen as a problem by the individual. More specifically, many preneurotic masochists do not see how their excessively self-sacrificing, other-oriented provocative, passive-aggressive behaviors and their avoidance of direct confrontation defeat their strivings for love, autonomy, and authentic relationships. On the other hand, preneurotic masochists may realize that their repetitive maladaptive relationship interactions are problematic, but they are unable to realize desired changes and thus feel lowered self-esteem as a result.

DIFFERENTIAL DIAGNOSIS OF PRENEUROTIC, BORDERLINE, AND NEUROTIC MASOCHISM

Clinicians need to be able to differentiate neurotic, preneurotic, and borderline levels of masochism. Treatment plans (including the type of corrective interpersonal experience) will vary depending not only on the type of character pathology that is presented by the patient, but also on the level of ego structure that the patient manifests. Horner (1979) believes that structural issues take treatment precedence over the type of character organization that is presented. In this section we describe more specifically the manifestations of masochism at the neurotic and borderline levels of ego organization and the differentiating criteria.

Neurotic Masochism

When the masochistic personality develops at the neurotic or oedipal level of ego structure, the individual demonstrates what Kernberg (1976) has identified as a stable, cohesive, well-integrated core identity, a clearly attained libidinal object constancy, and well-developed impulse control, frustration tolerance, and subliminatory functioning. These patients are also able to establish stable, well-differentiated, in-depth object relationships (Kernberg 1988). Regression for the neurotic masochist is at the psychosexual level, with the individual's ego or "friendly observer" remaining intact and accessible to ally with the therapist in exploring and understanding internal processes and transference phenomena.

The symptomatology (e.g., pathological altruism, painful self-criticism) of the neurotic masochist most clearly appears to serve as both payment and permission for forbidden, unacceptable oedipal desires and aggression. Freud (1924) stated that the sadistic superego needs to punish and the masochistic ego submits to punishments out of an excessive unconscious sense of guilt (Meyers

1988). The neurotic masochistic personality structure is characterized by reaction formations, depressive perfectionism, an excessively guilt-ridden but well-integrated moral conscience, an accentuated need for love and support, and fears around the expression of anger (Kernberg 1988).

Borderline Masochism

When the masochistic character is structured at the borderline level of object relations development, the individual demonstrates identity diffusion, vulnerability (under stress or the influence of alcohol or drugs) to brief psychotic episodes, more severe reality distortions, and primitive ego defenses, such as frequent and extreme use of splitting, projective identifications, denial, and omnipotence (Kernberg 1975, 1988). Poor impulse control, low frustration tolerance, and affective instability are also typical. Kernberg (1988) notes that borderline masochists (or sadomasochistic personality disorders) typically alternate "self-demeaning, self-debasing, self-humiliating behaviors with sadistic attacks" toward the same needed object. These individuals see themselves as "the victims of others' aggression, bitterly complain about their mistreatment; and adamantly justify their own aggressions toward those whom they are dependent on" (pp. 64–65). Overall, however, they demonstrate excessive dependency and clinging behaviors as opposed to the aloofness of the borderline narcissist.

The differences between borderline and neurotic masochism can be illustrated by two patients who each presented as other-oriented, investing their self-worth in taking care of others. They both appeared to blame themselves for the problems in their intimate relationships. Their presentations differed markedly, however, in terms of frustration tolerance, impulse control, level of neediness, and coercive attempts at object manipulation.

Mark, a 30-year-old white, homosexual male, presented with neurotic-level masochism. Mark manifested substantial unconscious guilt over his gay lifestyle, which his family's faith defined as sinful. He therefore tried hard to make up for his guilty pleasures through good works and doing for others. He took special satisfaction in fulfilling the requests of others to whom he was close when it meant a deprivation of his own needs.

In general, Mark felt driven by perfectionistic strivings and demands to be a nice guy. Overinhibited about his own needs, Mark had a hard time letting even his partner of five years know what he was needing in a straightforward manner. Because Mark exhibited difficulty in discriminating between important and unimportant requests, he treated all his partner's requests as if they were urgent demands to which he had to respond. Mark then tried to control feeling overwhelmed by periodically isolating himself in his work or by avoidance (e.g., not answering the phone). When his partner turned down a request of Mark's, however, Mark was generally very gracious and understanding. When Mark suffered, he believed that he deserved it as punishment for hurting his parents by being gay.

Susan, a 28-year-old white heterosexual female, manifested masochism structured at the borderline level of ego and object relations development. In general, Susan gave in relationships in order to get. When Susan was frustrated or disappointed by her partner, she catastrophized, felt "worthless and discarded like a used piece of Kleenex," and then vacillated between desperate attempts to coerce reassurance from him and sadistic attacks cloaked in self-denigrating, sulking communications.

For example, when her boyfriend left on a work assignment that took him across the country for a week, she felt abandoned. In an attempt to secure reassurance and feel whole again, she called him and left a message on his answering machine, knowing John would be checking it periodically. "I'm sorry, John, I know you're busy. Just give me a call when you get the chance . . . if you want to . . . if you're not too tired. I should be up. You know how I get when you're gone. Well, maybe this time I'll be okay. So just call if you want to."

When he did not call back right away, she began to feel a desperate clingy feeling and more panicked. She wondered if he was really working or if he were out on the town. She began calling him every 20 minutes and continued leaving messages over the next four hours until she took six sleeping pills and "passed out." Her messages became more and more interpenetrated with aggression, always starting out with an apology and ending with implied dire consequences if he did not respond to her. "I'm sorry, John. I don't want to bother you when you're obviously so busy, but I've been feeling so bad. I just got scared. I don't want to do anything stupid. I just feel so alone. Why does your work always come first? Call me. I feel like I don't matter and that if I died you wouldn't care anyway. Nevermind, I'll be okay."

Primary Differentiating Features

The primary differentiating features between preneurotic and borderline masochism remain structural. For example, while preneurotic masochists can resort to masochistic splitting if their primary security attachment is in jeopardy (e.g., by assigning blame to themselves and exonerating their love object), they do not generally use these mechanisms in other areas of their life or under daily circumstances. Furthermore, they do not generally experience their love objects as "all bad." In contrast, the ubiquitous use of splitting is one of the hallmarks of borderline pathology. While preneurotic masochists can often be experienced as irritating, passive-aggressive, and subtly provocative, they rarely, if ever, display the intense negative transference and directly hostile behaviors (e.g., self-mutilation, verbal attacks, suicidal acting out) so frequently observed in borderline patients.

However, diagnostic clarity between preneurotic and borderline masochism can be difficult. Gear and colleagues (1983) observe that borderline patients who are actually behaving sadistically may believe themselves to be acting masochistically in relationship to a sadistic other. Also self-destructive behaviors, even when manifest in extreme form, typically remain ego-syntonic for sadomasochistic personalities, while such behaviors typically remain at least partially ego-dystonic for the preneurotic masochist (Kernberg 1988).

Preneurotic masochism can be similarly differentiated from neurotic masochism through structural analysis. At the neurotic level of ego and object relations, the masochistic individual sustains clearly attained object and self constancy as well as a well-integrated, cohesive core identity. In contrast, at the preneurotic level, masochistic individuals manifest a relatively differentiated and cohesive sense of self or core identity, but demonstrate a weakness in self integration due to "masochistic splitting" (Meyers 1988) and a great fear of separation and loss (Avery 1977). Concomitantly, the preneurotic masochist demonstrates unstable object constancy related to the activation of masochistic splitting and the insufficiency of emotionally sustaining, self-soothing, transmuting internalizations. Once again, as a result of ensuing insecurity, preneurotic masochists remain overly dependent upon the idealized love object for their self-esteem and security needs.

Due to these structural weaknesses, masochistic symptomatology at the preneurotic level primarily serves security and self-esteem operations, whereas at the neurotic level such symptomatology primarily serves dynamic rather than structural motivations (e.g., punishment for guilty wishes or unacceptable impulses versus self-esteem or security operations). While the structural motivation for preneurotic masochists is thus similar to borderline ego organizations, the depth and range of ego and functional impairment are distinctively different. Preneurotic masochists have substantially more structural resources to call upon than do borderlines, although in both cases masochism serves as a linkage with a suffering parental selfobject in addition to maintaining the structural deficits.

This chapter discussed the structural and defensive hallmarks of preneurotic masochism and differentiated this intermediate level of masochism from more and less developmentally advanced manifestations of this pathology. These descriptions were preceded by a brief chronicle of the evolutionary context in which we proposed the construct of preneurotic masochism.

More specifically, the hallmarks of preneurotic masochism are the following structural issues: (a) failure to complete transmuting internalizations of realistic maternal functions (e.g., soothing, self-regard, confidence in problem solving), which results in (b) failure to complete object constancy; (c) defensive propensities toward masochistic splitting and masochistic triangulation; and (d) anxious attachment, which is related to both structural and defensive properties. Differential diagnosis between neurotic, preneurotic, and borderline masochism is most readily made on a structural basis and/or a functional analysis of the motivational impetus for the masochistic symptomology.

The following chapter describes in detail the factors involved in the etiology of preneurotic masochism. Throughout the remainder of this book, in fact, it will be assumed that the type of masochism referred to is the preneurotic level of ego and object relations development unless otherwise indicated.

5

Etiology of the Masochistic Personality

Like many personality disorders, the masochistic personality evolves from both a family system that imposes chronic mistreatment on the child as well as a nonoptimal resolution of particular developmental stages. More specifically, we believe masochism is associated with a childhood of prolonged hostility and deprivation as well as ephemeral, inconsistent moments of warmth that set up an intense longing for the lost "good" object. This chapter addresses both the general familial and particular developmental etiology of masochism and attempts to demonstrate how the preneurotic masochistic character traits described in Chapters 3 and 4 emerge from particular etiological patterns. It also discusses particular features of resiliency that prevent more serious pathology (e.g., narcissistic or borderline personality disorders).

GENERAL FAMILIAL PATTERNS IN THE DEVELOPMENT OF MASOCHISM

A number of general factors in the family of origin, some of which will be discussed in detail, may contribute to the development of masochistic character traits. These include (a) parental unpredictability, (b) insensitivity, (c) intrusiveness, (d) hypocrisy, (e) parental use of projective defenses, (f) scapegoating of the child, (g) parentification of the child, (h) inability to parent the child, and (i) infantalization of the child for illness and misbehavior. These general parental traits also have an impact upon the masochistic character through the manner that parents of masochists respond to the child during particular stages of development.

Unpredictability

The first general familial factor in the development of masochism is the experience of being raised in a chronically unpredictable environment (Glickauf-Hughes and Wells 1991) that is characterized by a preponderance of hostility and deprivation and a few golden moments of love and understanding. Due to ambivalence in parental attitudes (Bromberg 1955) as well as to parental egocentricity, children are frequently rewarded and punished for the same behavior.

In masochists' families, parental responses to children's needs, feelings, and behavior are often based more on the parent's moods than on signals from the child or on sound principles of child rearing. Such egocentricity often leads parents to behave in grossly unattuned ways toward their child. This contention is supported by Berliner

(1958), who believes that masochistic behavior is not caused by severe, overt cruelty toward children but by intense ambivalence toward the child that tends to be closer to the hostile side.

For example, one masochistic patient's narcissistic father sometimes praised him for his good grades (as it met his father's narcissistic needs). At other times his father felt envious of and competitive with his son's academic achievements and berated him for "being a bookworm and not playing ball more like the other boys." Another masochistic patient's alcoholic mother was able to be extremely loving and sensitive with her at important times. However, she became critical and abusive when she was drinking. A third patient's mother would dole out huge punishments for minor transgressions during a fit of rage. She would then remorsefully rescind them the next day. Needless to say, there is a high frequency of both substance abuse and borderline and narcissistic characteristics among parents of masochists.

Thus what appears to be punishment-seeking behavior or ambivalent attachment to "bad" objects may at least in part simply be behavior that is maintained by intermittent reinforcement from the environment. This contention is supported by several animal studies. For example, Azrin and Holz (1966) found that when pigeons were intermittently reinforced and then punished for the same behavior, they maintained a high level of responding. In an analogue study, Fisher (1955) demonstrated that puppies that were both rewarded and punished for approaching the experimenter exhibited greater dependency upon the experimenter than did the puppies in the 100 percent reward group. There are thus operant models in animal research for maintaining "masochistic" behavior in animals with intermittent schedules of reward and punishment, similarly to what parents of masochists are purported to do with their children (Glickauf-Hughes and Wells 1991).

Additional research evidence for the hypothesis that masochistic behavior results in part from parental inconsistency and insensitivity (as well as parental interference) is provided in a study by Ainsworth and colleagues (1969). In a study on attachment and exploratory behavior in 1-year-old children, the investigators found that mothers who were sensitive, warm, cooperative, and accepting had children who used them as a secure base from which they explored the environment. Mothers who were cold but didn't interfere with their child's play had children who were not approaching toward others but who exhibited a great deal of exploratory behavior. However, children whose mothers were inconsistently warm, insensitive, and interfering behaved in an ambivalently dependent manner toward others (i.e. alternated between clinging and hitting) and were not highly exploratory. This study has application to understanding the separation-individuation phase of development (which will be explored later in this chapter). It also points to the importance of parental intrusion upon masochistic development.

In this line of thought, Nydes (1963) found that what was significant in the family background of masochistic patients was not a pattern of harsh authority but rather the lack of consistent rational authority. Quite often parents of masochists are uncontrolled, controlling individuals who behave like tyrannical children. One patient as an adolescent locked himself in the bathroom to remove himself from his father's verbal attacks. The father became so enraged that he broke the door down.

Hypocrisy

While parents of masochists demonstrate a remarkable lack of control over their impulses (e.g., substance abuse, compulsive eating, child abuse), their children are expected to control their impulses and behavior before they are developmentally able to do so. Furthermore, parents of masochists frequently ask their children to do what they say rather than what they do. For example, one patient's mother (who consumed nothing during the day but black coffee and cigarettes) forced her son to eat a large breakfast. Another patient's father used to scream at him, "I don't want to hear another goddamn swear word out of your mouth" (Glickauf-Hughes and Wells 1991).

This discrepancy between what parents of masochists "practice" and what they "preach" was also noted by Bromberg (1955), who observed that mothers of masochists often present to the world as kind, self-sacrificing, and devoted but behave toward their child in an abusive and self-centered manner. For example, one patient who took care of her childlike, depressed mother since she was 5 years old said that everyone thought that her mother was a saint. In spite of this patient's solicitous behavior, her mother blamed her chronic depression on her child and frequently told her that she was "a punishment from God." Another patient's mother was a social pillar of the community. She used to severely berate her children on the way to church, and then pinch their cheeks before they arrived and thus enter church "looking like the perfect rosy-cheeked family." Although privately she once broke her son's arm in an outburst of temper and told him that if she had known he would turn out to be homosexual, she would have had an abortion, publicly she received a B'nai B'rith award for community service.

Children raised in these circumstances eventually learn to deny their own perceptions of their parents. Through the processes of introjection and identification, they come to believe that their parents behave in a negligent or hostile manner toward them because they are "bad" or in some way defective. "Identifying with one or both parents, [the child] reproaches himself as the one who is at fault, having exonerated his parents because their demands are supposedly appropriate. Their love is presumed to be available but withheld until he merits it" (Grand 1973, p. 446).

There are thus many reasons for children's illusions about their bad self and their good parent(s). Children are highly dependent upon their parents. Their need for their parents' love and their instinct for self-preservation thus motivates them to repress and deny perceptions of their parents that might cause them to be angry (Menaker 1953), as anger can translate into anticipated separation and loss. Furthermore, "no child cares to admit that his parents are gravely at fault. To recognize frankly that a mother's exploiting you for her own ends or that a father is unjust and tyrannical or that neither parent wanted you is intensely painful. Moreover, it is frightening" (Bowlby 1973, p. 316). Thus, to avoid potential loss and separation, children maintain their view of the parents as loving and good and attribute any frustration in the parent–child relationship to their own bad or defective self (Menaker 1953).

Scapegoating

Another contributor to the perceptual pattern of bad self/good object is the tendency of parents of masochists to defend against their own feelings of shame and low self-esteem through frequent blaming of their child. Bromberg (1955) observed that mothers of masochists make frequent use of defenses such as projection, denial, displacement, reaction formation, and rationalization, and often make "accusations of ingratitude and inconsiderateness aimed at lowering others' self-esteem" (p. 806). Grand (1973) notes that while parents of masochists demand a great deal from their children, they are never satisfied. Both parents and child agree that if there is a problem, it is the child's fault.

This pattern becomes exacerbated when the child is scapegoated in the family. Parents of masochists are often highly narcissistic and tend to assume what Klein (1935) described as the paranoid position (i.e., protection of self from bad objects). They thus have a tendency to idealize and devalue others and are prone to projecting the ego dystonic, "shameful" aspects of their self in order to protect their self-esteem. In some families, one child assumes the role of the parents' ideal self (or the "good" child) and another assumes the role of the parents' devalued self (or the "bad" child).

The assignment of the good-child role may be based on (a) sex (e.g., parent wanted a son), (b) birth order (e.g., parent likes to baby the youngest), (c) particular talents, or (d) the child's temperament being more compatible with the parent. The "bad child" role may similarly be assigned, based on (a) sex (e.g., parents devalue females), (b) birth order (e.g., child was born first and being the container of parent's negative projection was a necessary function), (c) lack of temperamental fit (e.g., active child with a sensitive or irritable mother), and (d) resemblance to a family member with whom the parent has a conflict.

Once the "bad" child is assigned the scapegoat role, the child's sense of identity as a bad person becomes rigidified. Furthermore, when the child observes the parent idealizing one of the other siblings, comparing the child to that sibling (unfavorably) and giving the "good child" the love that he or she desires, the illusion that the parent's love is available but withheld (as undeserved) becomes reinforced.

"Parentification" (Minuchin et al. 1967)

In addition to being the scapegoat, masochists commonly assume the role of parentified child in their families of origin. Due to their narcissism and immaturity, parents of masochists often use their children as objects for gratifying their own dependency needs and narcissistic needs rather than attending to the child's evolving developmental needs and concerns. Bromberg (1955) believes that "because the child represents a parental figure in the mother's unconscious, the demands upon him for all types of gratification seem appropriate to her or at least so tempting that she succumbs to them" (p. 802).

Masochists can be parentified in their families in two ways. They may assume the role of the parent's selfobject. In this role, the child develops "an amazing capacity to perceive and respond intuitively, that is unconsciously to the needs of the mother" (Miller 1981, p. 8), thus providing the narcissistic functions for the mother (e.g., empathy, mirroring, soothing) that she is unable to provide for herself. By providing selfobject functions for the parent, the child attains a measure of love and security for him- or herself (Miller 1981).

One patient who manifested this dynamic was considered her mother's best friend. As a child, her mother frequently confided in her daughter about marital difficulties, seeking a listening ear, understanding, and comfort from her. This patient felt responsible for keeping her mother "propped up" so that her mother (the more functional parent) would continue to provide for her. As an adult, this patient became a psychotherapist and frequently assumed the role of comforting good listener with her colleagues and friends.

A second parental role that masochists often take in their family of origin is that of caretaker. At a young age, masochists learn to competently assume the responsibilities that their immature and unreliable parents are unable to handle. At $2\frac{1}{2}$ years old, one patient became the mother of her newborn sister as her "mother didn't really like babies." Another patient (at age 4) helped her mother clean up after her alcoholic father. A third patient used to wake her mother up for work every morning so that she wouldn't lose her job.

Inadequate Parenting

While parents of masochists assign excessive responsibility to their children, they demonstrate severely limited abilities to prepare their children for autonomous adult functioning. These parents often have a surprising lack of skills for independent functioning (e.g., inability to drive a car, problems maintaining a budget). They also have insufficient knowledge about appropriate parenting. Parents of masochists demonstrate extreme ignorance about how to reinforce appropriate behavior and how to use calm, rational persuasion. Instead, parents of masochists tend to resort to extreme measures to control their child, including shaming, excessive guilt, physical abuse, and punishments that are out of proportion to the infraction. One patient's mother told her that she couldn't go to the prom because she hadn't done her chores that day. Another patient's father induced guilt by telling him that he would "give me a heart attack and kill me" when he thought the patient was disrespectful.

Menaker (1953) also observed that some mothers of masochists compensate for their lack of genuine maternal feelings by infantalizing and overprotecting their children. For example, one 40-year-old masochistic patient reported that his mother still called him by his baby name, "lamb chops." Another patient's father said that he would buy her a car if she stayed home and didn't go away to college, thus depriving the child of the necessary opportunities and encouragement to become genuinely independent.

As a result of their parents' high expectations, infantalization, and inadequate teaching of skills for autonomous functioning, masochists often develop a sense of pseudomaturity or a persona of competence with an underlying feeling of being markedly unprepared for the world. As a result of having to raise themselves and receiving mixed messages about their ability from their parents, they often feel like impostors. For example, one patient who was quickly promoted to the vice presidency of her company lived in constant fear that her underlying inadequacy would be discovered.

In addition to failing to impart adult skills to their children, parents of masochists are often so self-absorbed that their children are only able to gain their attention through misbehavior (Berliner 1947) or by becoming physically ill (Panken 1983). These patients often come to believe that they are most loved when suffering (Panken 1983). For example, one patient, whose borderline mother threatened suicide and was in and out of mental hospitals since the patient was 5, was only able to get attention from her family when she began to have panic attacks herself.

Grand (1973) believes that the pity that masochists receive from their parents when suffering becomes confused with love. However, receiving pity for suffering rather than love for genuine self-expression further solidifies the masochist's sense of having a bad or defective self. This dynamic thus has a severely debilitating effect upon the child's self-esteem.

Identification with a Masochistic Parent

A final general factor in the etiology of masochism is the process of identifying with a masochistic or inadequate parent. It has been observed that masochistic patients often identify with a masochistic parent of the same sex, and, as children, masochists become caught in the cross fire of accusations between parents. For example, one patient's father told him that he was overly sensitive, just as his mother was, while his mother told him that he was too impulsive, just as his father was.

Grand (1973) additionally noted that the same sex parent of the masochist is often viewed as having serious shortcomings. The parent may also feel an underlying sense of envy toward or competition with the child when he or she does succeed. For example, one patient's father (who had secret intellectual aspirations) would get angry and rejecting toward his son when he made good grades at school. Another patient reported that while her mother was sympathetic with her lack of social success as a child, when she became a popular adolescent, her mother seemed to resent her and frequently mocked her boy-friends.

Masochists thus learn as children to undermine their own competencies rather than to show up their parents. They come to fear success (because of the potential envy it may inspire in others) as well as failure (because of the potential criticism it may inspire in others).

SPECIFIC DEVELOPMENTAL ISSUES IN THE ETIOLOGY OF MASOCHISM

As will be discussed in Chapter 6, all character disorders result from a mishandling (or at least a nonoptimal handling) of particular developmental stages by the significant others in a child's life. As a consequence, children may manifest particular unresolved developmental issues that continue to trouble them in adult life (e.g., lack of trust, problems with separation, undeveloped sense of self). We now examine how the masochistic character emerges through various phases of the developmental sequence.

Symbiosis

During the first stage of development referred to as the symbiotic stage by Mahler and colleagues (1975) and as the basic trust versus mistrust stage by Erikson (1950), the child develops an attachment to objects and learns whether or not he or she can reliably depend upon them to get his or her needs for love, attention, and basic security met. Unlike the schizoid personality, whose parents are so remote and emotionally unavailable that the child fails to make an adequate symbiotic attachment (Johnson 1985), the significant objects of masochists have some capacity for emotional engagement. The authors have particularly noted a pattern in which the parents or alternate objects (e.g., grandparents, siblings) of masochists were able to respond more appropriately to an infant but had a more difficult time parenting a toddler or older child.

However, while parents of masochists have some capacity for emotional engagement, their own depressed (Bromberg 1955) or narcissistic (Grand 1973) character causes the nurturing that they are able to provide for their child to be very erratic. Parents of masochists are frequently unempathic and alternate between being neglectful and overinvolved. Thus, while the child gets enough needs gratified to make an attachment to objects, he or she experiences substantial maternal deprivation. As a result, the child feels chronically needful and eventually learns to deny his or her dependency needs. As adults, masochists frequently manifest a number of oral character traits that result from both experiencing deprivation and defending against it. These include (a) accentuated neediness (often unconscious), (b) lack of awareness about their dependency needs, (c) difficulty asking for or receiving help, (d) fear of being abandoned, and (e) an overnurturing of others. The latter process occurs as a result of the displacement and projection of the masochist's dependency needs upon others combined with identification with their gratification (Johnson 1985). Thus in the first developmental stage, the child gets enough dependency needs met to make an attachment but not enough to make a secure attachment.

Separation-Individuation

In the second developmental stage referred to by Mahler and colleagues (1975) as separation-individuation and Erikson (1950) as autonomy versus shame and doubt, the child faces a number of developmental tasks: (a) being able to tolerate separations, (b) developing a sense of self, and (c) regulating self-esteem.

With regard to the first goal (mastering separation anxiety), due to the parent's overinvolvement and intrusiveness (when the parent is needful) and infantalization of the child, the parent has some tendency to disrupt the child's natural urges to explore the world. This may contribute to both a sense of frustration and fearfulness. Thus, for example one very competent, tenured university professor had a mild chronic illness as a child. Her parents restricted her age-appropriate activities with peers. As an adolescent, they discouraged her from learning to drive and as a young adult prevented her from attending an Ivy

League school (to which she was accepted). As an adult, in spite of her realistic capabilities, she experienced occasional separation anxiety and several phobias.

Furthermore, due to the parent's unpredictability, the child doesn't often enough experience the parent as a secure base to return to for refueling. Combined, both factors contribute to the child developing an anxious attachment to objects. This contributes to the difficulty that masochistic patients have separating from their love objects as adults. This pattern is then further reinforced by a tendency on the part of parents to use punishing withdrawal as a means of controlling their children.

However, while parents of masochists are often very self-involved, tend to use their children narcissistically, and don't provide optimal mirroring, they are not totally symbiotic with their children and are thus able to tolerate more individuation in their children than is observed among borderline and narcissistic personalities. Parents of masochists often experience some relief (as well as anxiety) when their children reach the practicing phase and become less dependent upon them. They thus have greater tolerance for the child's engagement in transitional activities (e.g., independent play) and relationships with others than is tolerated by mothers of borderline personalities. Separation-individuation is additionally promoted by the process of parental scapegoating, which establishes the child's identity as different from (albeit worse than) his or her parents. For example, one masochistic patient who was devalued by his mother (due to his effeminate behavior and resemblance to his father) was the only sibling who did not develop a borderline or narcissistic character structure. His brother, who was idealized by the mother and used as her narcissistic object, became a drug dealer.

Another factor in the development of masochism involves crushing the child's will. For example, one masochistic patient described a morning ritual of her mother attempting to force her to eat oatmeal. Johnson (1985) believes that the "crushing of the will experienced by masochists occurs when the child begins to assert her will and claims her right to be independent" (p. 51). However, as this disruption occurs at a somewhat later time ("on the way to object constancy") in the masochist than the derailed individuation process of the borderline or narcissistic personality (during hatching through rapprochement), the masochist has a better chance of developing and consolidating a sense of self. This provides the child with a greater capacity to resist parental domination when it occurs. Thus, this patient waited until her mother was distracted and threw the oatmeal in the garbage. Johnson believes, however, that as the child is dependent upon the parent and the parent inevitably has greater power, the child must eventually capitulate to the parent's will. He or she does so, however, with great suppressed resentment leading to the masochistic pattern of overt compliance and covert deviance (e.g., help-rejecting complaining). This pattern is one of the self-defeating ways that masochists struggle to individuate from the objects in their lives.

Masochists thus emerge from the separation-individuation stage with a sense of anxious attachment to their objects, some problems with separation, a reasonably developed sense of self, and some problems with autonomy. The latter leads to both a tendency toward willfulness and to struggles between compliance and defiance. Thus, the patient in the previous example would only order cheeseburgers when she went to restaurants.

Of greatest importance, masochists emerge from the separation-individuation stage with significant deficits in the foundation for what later becomes healthy self-esteem. As previously described, for defensive purposes, parents of masochists tend to be highly critical and make extensive use of projection and projective identification. However, children are highly dependent upon the parents that devalue or abuse them and thus must find the means to deal with this painful reality so that they feel safe.

Fairbairn (1943) proposed that masochists cope with this painful reality by setting up a "moral defense against bad objects" by internalizing the abusive parent or primary other in order to feel more control and gain "outer security." "By internalizing the burden of badness" (p. 65), which really resides in the object, the masochist seeks to eliminate the object's badness and thus assures a sense of outer security that depends upon having good objects. This process of attaining the illusion of outer security often results in the undesirable presence of internalized bad objects. "Outer security is . . . purchased at the price of inner security . . . [and the] ego is henceforth left at the mercy of . . . internal . . . persecutors, against which defenses have to be, first hastily erected, and later laboriously consolidated" (p. 65). Thus, to feel more secure the child comes to believe that the badness in the object resides in him- or herself. This defense, however, takes a great toll on the masochist's self-esteem.

A second developmental factor in the development of poor self-esteem involves the use of "masochistic splitting" (Meyers 1988). As the preneurotic masochistic character described in this book emerges at the stage in object relations in which good and bad aspects of objects are integrated but good and bad aspects of the self are not, masochists tend to protect the relationship with the object through splitting or devaluing the self. Mollinger (1982) believes that "in the face of the bad object, [the masochist] will split off the bad to maintain the relationship with the good" (p. 384). Because of the preponderance of parental ill-will, the masochistic's self-integration is stymied. Continuing to rely on masochistic splitting to preserve the relationship with the object, however, hurts the masochist's developing self-esteem.

In conclusion, masochism results from parent–child struggles during the early stages of development causing the child to be vulnerable in the areas of autonomy, self-esteem, and separation. These areas are further impaired by chronic parental behaviors such as blaming, hypocrisy, controllingness, unpredictability, and continued narcissistic use of the child.

DIFFERENTIAL ETIOLOGY OF PRENEUROTIC MASOCHISM

We contend that preneurotic masochism results from specific experiences with objects over time (e.g., parentification, unpredictability, scapegoating, intrusiveness) and during particular developmental phases (e.g., sporadic gratification of dependency needs during the symbiotic phase). Some of the chronic relational and specific developmental patterns such as inconsistency and parental narcissism are also associated with the borderline and narcissistic personality. Therefore, the etiological differences between these three disorders will be briefly addressed.

While families of hysteroid borderlines and masochists are often inconsistent, abusive, and unpredictable, parents of masochists generally support the child's attempts at separation-individuation more than parents of the borderline child. One masochistic patient described her mother's support for her participation in subliminatory activities that helped give her ample opportunity to establish a transitional space. She reported many fond memories of drawing and painting with her mother busy in another room.

Masochists also report less punishing withdrawal and more support for peer relationships than do borderline patients. For example, one borderline patient reported that her mother became ill every time she went away to camp (at her father's urging). In contrast, one masochistic patient remembers spending a great deal of time playing with peers. Another frequently walked over to visit her grandparents.

We have not, however, noted a difference in the amount of abuse experienced by borderline and masochistic patients. Rather, a marked difference exists in the promotion of separation-individuation (and autonomous ego functions) and more positive object relations experiences with non-parent figures in the histories of masochists.

In a similar vein, strong narcissistic tendencies have been noted in parents of both masochistics and narcissists. We have observed, however, a tendency in narcissistic families to consistently reinforce the narcissist for false self behavior that the parent condones. In masochistic families, parents are more unpredictable. Reinforcement of valued behaviors in the child is thus contingent upon the parent's mood.

Furthermore, narcissists tend to assume the role of idealized object in the family (e.g., the hero, the good one, the prodigy). Parents of narcissists tend to project their ego ideal on the child and identify with it. For example, one narcissistic patient (whose mother was obese) had her daughter modeling and restricted her diet from age 4. One wall in the house was covered with her professional photographs. Another narcissistic patient said his parents preserved his "bedroom like a shrine" in which football jackets and college degrees were displayed.

In contrast, masochists tend to be scapegoats and/or caretakers in their families. In the former role, parents project the "bad" aspects of themselves upon the child or create in the child (through projective identification) the aspects of their personality that are ego-dystonic. In the role of caretaker, the child is used for responding to parental and sibling needs. Both roles, however, do not suppress development of the child's true self to the extent that the role of ideal object does. Masochists tend to know more about what they really feel and want than narcissists. They tend, however, to feel extremely ashamed of their emotions and their needs.

RESILIENCY FACTORS IN PRENEUROTIC MASOCHISM

A challenging puzzle in understanding the etiology of masochism is why children who have had such difficult lives are able to develop into adults who, although insecure, have considerable strengths (e.g., sense of self, ability to love, good functioning in many areas of their lives). The stories of abuse among masochistic patients are startling. There are numerous examples throughout this book of severe shaming and broken bones over minor transgressions. Yet most of these patients have long-term committed primary relationships (however conflictual), have no history of psychotic episodes, function well at work, are not abusive toward others, and despite suicidal ideation have few instances of actual suicide attempts. As a means of explaining this diagnostic puzzle, the resiliency factors that may contribute to better social-emotional functioning of masochistic (than borderline and narcissistic) patients, in spite of severe abuse histories, will be addressed. These resiliency factors will be a further elaboration on some patterns alluded to in discussing differential etiology of masochistic, narcissistic, and borderline patients. They include (a) the use of alternative objects, and (b) the ability to constructively use fantasy and subliminatory channels.

Use of Alternative Objects

A common finding in the literature on resiliency is a history of finding good relationships with people other than their parents (Lieberman 1982, Rutter 1986). This may be due to some biological predisposition toward extrovertism, to the presence of alternative objects in the child's life, and to the parent's support of the child's relationships with those objects. Thus, one patient from an early age was more involved in peer relationships than with her parents. Her first truly secure, trusting relationship occurred at age 11 with a same-sex chum. Another patient regarded her grandparents as her "real" parents and experienced more of a sense of loss at their death than at her father's death. Another patient recalled that at age 5 he frequently spent time with a neighbor and her family. These types of self reports contrast markedly with those of patients with a more borderline organization. By having other sources of caring and affection, these children were better able to separate and had alternative identification figures and models for relationships.

Constructive Use of Fantasy and Subliminatory Channels

While masochistic patients were able to find alternative objects, most did not adequately get their dependency needs met. Many, however, learned to use fantasy as a means of imagining better relationships with others and happier lives. Furthermore, as in Beardslee's (1989) study of resilient individuals, masochistic patients tended to translate their ideals into actions. Thus, rather than living in a world of ideas as schizoid patients are prone to do, they tend to try to make their wishes reality. One patient persisted in her attempts to be popular until she succeeded. Another (despite significant learning disabilities and problems at school as an adolescent) got her G.E.D. and eventually her Ph.D. Often these patients had one adult in their life who encouraged self-efficacy. For example, one patient's father gave him Norman Vincent Peale's book, *The Power of Positive Thinking,* when he was having problems with his girlfriend at age 13.

Furthermore, as alluded to in the previous section, many of these patients, from early on, made much use of subliminatory activity. One patient was heavily involved in sports. Another painted, wrote poetry, played the piano, and read piles of library books. This may have occurred as a result of both natural abilities in the child (e.g., talents, intelligence) and the parents' support of the child's participation in transitional activities. In contrast to narcissistic patients, these activities were predominantly conflict-free areas and not used to vicariously provide narcissistic gratification for their parents.

Through finding and pursuing relationships with alternative objects, imagining a happier life with more satisfying objects, and using subliminatory activities, the masochist is better able to relate to others, and to separate and individuate than might be expected given the repeated traumatic incidents in their histories. As in Beardslee's (1989) study of resilient individuals, they tend to view the future "with hope albeit a 'troubled' hope" (p. 275).

Thus, narcissistic parents may use children for different functions, leading to different character develop-

ment. When children are used as a repository of parents'
bad self experience, they tend to become more masochistic
or depressive. When used to meet parents' ego ideal needs,
the child may develop a progressive narcissistic style.
When the child is used to meet selfobject functions (e.g.,
empathy, admiration, soothing) for the parent, the child
often develops regressive narcissistic or masochistic character traits. Differential diagnoses between the last two
styles can be a difficult task.

6

Object Relations Therapy

While object relations theory is becoming an influential perspective in contemporary clinical work as a means of understanding patients (particularly those with narcissistic and borderline disorders), until recently, its main impact upon treatment has been limited to the modification of traditional psychoanalytic technique (Cashdan 1988). Greenson (1967), for example, posits that while what is curative in treatment is the interpretation of transference, in order to interpret transference, a working alliance must first exist between analyst and patient. Kleinian analysts believe that the manner in which interpretations are made can transform the relationship between patient and analyst (Greenberg and Mitchell 1983). Rucker (1968) similarly stresses that in interpreting the transference, analysts implicitly say to patients that they are not like their bad objects but are trying to understand them and to reach them. Pine (1993) believes that an "interpretation can have its maximum effect because the relationship (non-condemning) belies the patient's inner world" and that "additionally, the relationship factor has its maximum effect at precisely the moment of interpretation" (pp. 192–193).

In contrast, Sullivan (1953) de-emphasizes the value of interpretation altogether. Rather, he highlights the importance of the analyst as a new relationship in the patient's life. Fairbairn (1952) stresses the necessity of the analyst's becoming a good object in order to provide the patient with sufficient security to relinquish bad object ties. Kohut (1977) likewise believes that it is the actual interpersonal experience with the analyst that carries the treatment's therapeutic action. Furthermore, he suggests that specific analyst behaviors (e.g., empathizing, explaining, interpreting, mirroring, idealizing) are required as a corrective experience to heal the patient's developmental deficits. Guntrip (1961) states that in order to help patients, therapists must actually be the kind of person with whom patients can integrate their disparate fragments. Jacobs (1993) believes that while "many factors go into the development of rapport between patient and therapist including the matching of personalities and styles, employing the correct techniques of working from the surface down, tuning in to the patient's affects and interpreting these before one gets into deeper conflicts," these factors "will not be effective or have meaning if the basic ingredient, the *mensch* factor ingredient is not present" (pp. 4–5). Jacobs defines a mensch as a genuinely "mature individual with sound values who can relate warmly and empathically to another human being" (p. 4). The concept of a "corrective emotional experience" as outlined by Alexander and French (1946) has, however, received substantial criticism within the analytic community. Alexander defined the corrective emotional experience in terms of the patient's reliving original traumatic experiences in the presence of a significant other (therapist, friend) with a more favorable resolution than in the original childhood conflict. Alexander recommended that the therapist "manipulate" the transference by assuming a role that would most readily evoke this corrective emotional experience (Horner 1979).

Greenson (1967) cautioned against the use of essentially manipulative and antianalytic techniques, pointing out that when such techniques are employed, "the patient does not learn to recognize and understand his resistances and there is no premium on insight as a means of overcoming resistances, there is no attempt to change the ego structure" (p. 136). Horner (1991), agreed, noting that, "antianalytic procedures can block or lessen the patient's capacity for insight and understanding" (p. 191).

The concept of a corrective emotional experience, however, seems to be experiencing a resurgence at this time. Renik (1993) discusses how an analyst's countertransference enactment can provide a corrective emotional experience that helps the patient to "recreate and master crucial pathogenic experiences" (p. 142). Furthermore, Norcross (1993) and Lazarus (1993) discuss tailoring therapeutic relationship stances to the patient's needs. Dolan and colleagues (1993) stress the importance of making the therapist's interpersonal stance contingent upon the patient's attachment style. Mahrer (1993) believes that crucial parts of the therapy relationship are uniquely tailored by and for each patient in each session. Finally, Weiss (1993) believes that patients seek corrective emotional experiences through their testing of the therapist and that therapists should provide patients with the experiences that they seek. Weiss further believes that providing these experiences helps patients to disprove their pathogenic beliefs and, thus, to pursue important but forbidden goals.

We do not conceptualize the therapist's offering of a corrective emotional experience as a manipulation or even as a role assumption, but rather as a genuine engagement that emphasizes the particular aspects of relationship that a specific patient has insufficiently received and that are required to facilitate healing or to help the patient work through an impasse. Much of the analytic community has recognized the validity of altering the analytic frame of neutral therapeutic abstinence for borderline patients who need the therapist to behave in a more warm, empathic, and authentic manner as well as to provide psychic functions these patients cannot provide for themselves (e.g., self-validation, self-soothing, selfobject differentiation). We believe that therapists may be more effective by altering their stance with other patients as well.

This proposal finds support in Lazarus's concept of the therapist as an "authentic chameleon." Lazarus thinks "it is important for the therapist to modify his or her participation in the therapeutic process in order to offer the most appropriate form of treatment for the client being seen as opposed to the situation where the therapist fits the person to the treatment" (Dryden 1991, pp. 17–18).

We believe that clinicians who utilize object relations theories to direct psychotherapy need to develop models of treatment that go beyond the mere modification of classical psychoanalytic technique and instead specify the precise nature in which the therapist must be a new object for each patient, given their particular characterological makeup. While Kohut (1977) has proposed such a model, self psychology best serves as a corrective interpersonal experience for individuals suffering from narcissistic disturbances (Hedges 1983).

We are not advocating "acting," "role playing," or being a "narcissistic object" for patients. What is suggested is tailoring the therapeutic relationship to the patient's developmental and interpersonal needs within the confines of what the therapist is authentically able to provide for the patient. All therapists have limits. Therapists with schizoid tendencies may not be able to help schizoid patients learn to bond. Therapists with borderline mothers may have particular difficulty containing the projective identifications of their borderline patients. What is important to note is that therapists do not help patients resolve transference feelings when they behave like the patients' internal objects. It is thus helpful for therapists to be aware of their strengths and limitations, their own countertransference issues, and to know which patients should be referred to another therapist.

CURRENT INTERPERSONAL AND OBJECT RELATIONS THEORIES OF TREATMENT

The most thorough model to date of a theory of object relations therapy that deals with varied patient problems has been proposed by Cashdan (1988). The basic tenets of Cashdan's model of object relations therapy are that (a) emphasis in treatment is placed on the therapist–patient relationship, (b) the therapist focuses upon the therapist–patient relationship in the here and now rather than on transference, defense mechanisms, and insight, and (c) the goal of therapy is to use the therapist–patient relationship as a vehicle for the patient's developing both healthier object relations and a more positive sense of self. Cashdan believes that interpersonal psychopathology is expressed through different projective identifications (e.g., dependency, power, sexuality, ingratiation) and that therapists can understand patients' pathology as well as derive a therapeutic strategy for treating that pathology by understanding their own countertransference reactions to the patient's projective identifications. Once therapists understand the patient's metacommunicative demands (e.g. "Take care of me," "Do what I say"), they can treat the patient's interpersonal pathology by refusing to concede or conform to the metacommunicative demand.

This strategy appears to be similar to that proposed by interpersonal therapists who stress the importance of the therapist's not responding in a complementary fashion to the patient but instead providing the patient with an "asocial response" (Beir 1966). The basic modes of the asocial response are (a) delay of response, (b) reflection of content and feeling, (c) labeling the style of interaction, and (d) making a paradigmatic response (Young and Beier 1982).

The primary limitation of this approach is that while it is recommended that therapists not make complementary, social responses to the patient's pathological and interpersonally self-defeating behaviors, and while alternate behaviors are recommended, there are no well-differentiated models that articulate well-developed repertoires of therapeutic responses that are geared specifically toward particular dysfunctional patterns of behaviors (e.g., behaving in a more spontaneous and emotional way with obsessive-compulsive clients and being more logical and cognitive with hysterical clients). Alternative strategies have been proposed by Leary (1957) and Benjamin (1979). In Benjamin's structural analysis of social behavior (SASB) model (1979), the therapist both refrains from emitting complementary behaviors and attempts to do the antithesis with the patient. For example, if the patient whines, defends, and justifies, the therapist confirms that the patient is acceptable just as he or she is. Through confirmation, it is hoped that the patient's defensiveness will give way to free and enthusiastic disclosure.

While Benjamin (1979, 1993) recommends therapeutic strategies tailored to modify particular dysfunctional behaviors of patients, this approach does not, however, specifically address the more complicated remediation of developmental deficits, including the building of new psychic structures. Thus the issue of increasing the development of an integrated sense of self is not addressed in the differential treatment of the dependent behavior of the borderline patient (who requires greater therapist involvement and support) from that of the hysteric (who requires therapeutic abstinence and the promotion of regression while recognizing the patient's real capabilities).

Developmental issues are more clearly addressed in the model of psychotherapy (based upon object relations and ego psychology principles) used by Althea Horner (1979, 1991). While Horner does not specifically systematize the particular therapeutic behaviors appropriate for the resolution of specific developmental failures (and their resultant character pathology), she does discuss different treatment implications relevant to patients with differential pathology.

For example, in discussing the tasks of treatment in working with a schizoid patient (whose developmental failure is seen as stemming from the symbiotic stage and the hatching phases of separation-individuation), Horner (1979) states: "one must provide a matrix of relatedness so that, as differentiation proceeds, it is not equated with object loss, with its danger of dissolution of the self" (pp. 92–93). In contrast, Horner discusses a borderline patient with rapprochement issues who expressed a premature wish to leave treatment. Horner believes that the appropriate stance in this case was to support the patient's separation-individuation striving symbolized in the wish to leave rather than confronting the wish as a resistance to treatment.

In her discussion of treatment for these two patients, Horner thus implicitly suggests that different types of corrective interpersonal experiences are needed for personality disorders that have developmental arrests at different stages. For the schizoid patient who received an inadequate symbiotic experience and consequently struggles with painful underattachment, Horner's therapeutic strategy is one of emotional availability. For the borderline patient who wasn't permitted to separate during rapprochement and consequently struggles with painful overattachment, the appropriate therapeutic strategy is one of supporting the patient's attempts at separation. Horner's (1991) most recent book, *Psychoanalytic Object Relations Therapy*, considers the application of object relations theory to the general themes and phases of the treatment process as applied to patients with various developmental deficits. However, she only briefly refers to therapeutic issues that are differentially relevant to patients with various character disorders (e.g., narcissistic, schizoid, depressive, paranoid).

In this chapter, an extended model of object relations therapy is presented. This model (a) gives greater specificity to the concept of providing patients with a new object or corrective interpersonal experience than previously described by Fairbairn, Sullivan, or Alexander and French; (b) takes developmental deficits and structural change into account more than does Benjamin's SASB model; (c) discusses proactive strategies for dealing with particular character disorders more than does Cashdan's model; and (d) further expands upon the therapeutic strategies for remediating developmental deficits as articulated by Horner (1979, 1991).

OBJECT RELATIONS THERAPY:
AN EXTENDED MODEL

The model of object relations therapy described in this chapter both draws upon and expands some of the previously explicated premises. The basic tenets of this theory of therapy are as follows. Character is seen as shaped by the interaction of the individual with significant others (Fairbairn 1952, Sullivan 1953). Particular importance is given to the interaction with others during critical periods of social and emotional development as described by Erikson (1950) and Mahler and colleagues (1975). As a result of these interpersonal experiences, individuals more or less successfully master major developmental tasks (e.g., basic trust, attachment, autonomy, separation-individuation).

Over the course of the first five years of life, residues from significant developmental/ interpersonal experiences become organized into a mental template of a representation of self in relationship to the important early significant others or objects in one's life. This template influences both the individual's phenomenological experience and his or her interpersonal behavior. An individual's mental template also predisposes him or her to assume a particular interpersonal stance such as moving toward, away from, or against others (Horney 1939) or friendly dominance, hostile dominance, friendly submission, or hostile submission (Leary 1957). From this perspective, character disorders are viewed as a manifestation of a dysfunctional mental template of interpersonal relationships resulting from specific developmental deficits causing the individual to assume a rigid and nonadaptive interpersonal stance.

Object relations therapy thus attempts to provide patients with the opportunity for a corrective interpersonal experience geared to help them to (a) modify their mental template of self and objects, (b) better master unresolved developmental issues, and (c) assume more varied and flexible interpersonal stances that are more appropriately attuned to their current social reality. By offering patients opportunities for corrective experiences, these patients are thus given "a developmental second chance" (Greenberg and Mitchell 1983, p. 356). The kind of corrective interpersonal relationship that a given patient requires varies with his or her particular developmental impasse, interpersonal stance, and resulting character disorder. The impact of this experience depends, in part, on a patient's ability to internalize.

For example, hysteroid borderlines tend to have unresolved separation-individuation issues resulting from failures during the rapprochement subphase of development (Masterson 1981). During rapprochement, hysteroids' maternal objects frequently withdrew emotional supplies in response to their children's separation and individuative strivings (Masterson 1981). With regard to their mental templates, hysteroids manifest (a) a weakened psychological boundary or separation between self and object representations, (b) insufficient integration of good and bad aspects of self and object representations, and (c) a preponderance of negative versus positive affects. As a result hysteroid borderlines rely on good/bad splitting, and thus tend to vacillate between clinging to objects perceived as "all good" or raging against objects perceived as "all bad." Therapeutic goals for hysteroid patients would thus involve helping them to (a) learn to psychologically separate self from others, (b) resolve splitting (Kernberg 1975), (c) become more genuinely self-activating (Masterson 1981), and (d) develop stabilized object constancy (Wells and Glickauf-Hughes 1986).

As a general guideline to the type of experience required for mastery of a given developmental stage, therapists are advised to (a) understand the principles used by good-enough parents to help children with particular developmental tasks and (b) adapt these principles to the therapeutic situation. The therapist must be careful not to infantilize or condescend to the adult patient with this approach. These principles can be very helpful as guides to treatment, however. For example, in the case of the hysteroid borderline patient, the therapist (like the good-enough rapprochement-phase parent) may best function as a "secure base from which to explore" (Ainsworth et al. 1969), serving as a constant object while supporting self-activation.

A second example illustrating this model is the case of the masochistic patient who struggles with anxious attachment as a result of chronic lack of attunement and unpredictability of caretakers (Glickauf-Hughes and Wells 1991). As developmental research suggests that empathic caretakers raise more securely attached children (Egeland and Farber 1985), empathy in psychotherapy may be an important tool for remediation with masochistic patients.

At this point, the question of the therapist's importance needs to be addressed. For example, why does the therapist matter so much to patients and how can the therapist's person potentially have such an enormous impact in helping patients overcome their development deficits? First, we agree with Fairbairn (1952) and Sullivan (1940) that the primary human motivation is the need to relate to others. Second character-disordered individuals often are not able to create or internalize a corrective experience outside of therapy with a trained clinician due to their own resistances or the power of their defenses.

We believe that individuals attempt to repair early trauma and correct developmental deficits through their primary relationships. However, due to repetition compulsions (i.e., repeating similar poor object choices), ego structural deficits (i.e., lack of frustration tolerance), and the fact that significant others have their own needs and their own developmental deficits to rectify, new relationships often repeat rather than heal old psychological wounds.

Because of their commitment to understanding their own countertransference and appropriately meeting patients' developmental needs, therapists are in an ideal position for offering corrective relationship opportunities. Furthermore, "the sheer intimacy and intensity of the relationship from the patient's side, deriving from the frequency, reliability, and isolation of the contacts, and deriving also from the patient's self-exposure through free association in an inherently unequal relationship, guarantees in most instances that the analyst will matter to the patient—immensely" (Pine 1993, p. 190).

Finally, a corrective interpersonal experience is seen as additive to rather than substitutive for interpretation. Insight resulting from correct interpretation provides patients with greater clarity and thus better ego-strength, including better reality testing. Insight is thus seen as enhancing psychological structure, including consolidation of the self (Kohut 1977). Thus, while insight is not seen as sufficient for change, it can greatly facilitate the process of mastering developmental deficits.

Table 6–1 offers an articulation of this model of object relations therapy with six personality disorders at three levels of ego development. Each personality disorder is examined with regard to stage of developmental arrest, treatment by significant others, resulting developmental failure, structural defects, and interpersonal stance. Based upon these deficits, therapeutic goals and corrective interpersonal experiences are formulated. Personality disorders are grouped according to level of ego development due to the commonalities in treatment priorities appropriate for individuals at similar levels of ego/object relation structure. For example, with neurotic patients, uncovering of repressed material/memories via therapeutic abstinence and promotion of regression is given priority. Encouraging transmuting internalization of specific ego is recommended with preneurotic clients and developing self and object constancy is the focus when working with borderline clients. Specific differences in treatment strategies are recommended, however, for clients within similar levels of ego development who have received differential treatment by objects and have developed different defensive and personality styles. For example, as illustrated by Horner (1979), it is recommended that therapists facilitate greater attachment in schizoid borderlines who never experienced an adequate symbiosis and encourage greater autonomy in hysteroid borderlines whose attempts at separation-individuation were generally unsupported.

It is not our intention to specify all aspects of treatment for these disorders. Nor is it implied that this model would be inappropriate for other personalities (e.g. paranoid, depressive). Rather, the goal is to begin to operationalize the model of object relations therapy described in this chapter so that clinicians who subscribe to object relations principles can systematically begin to integrate these formulations into their treatment strategies.

We are not advocating a "cookbook" approach to treatment (e.g., if a patient meets *DSM-IV* criteria for schizoid personality, the therapist should "act" engaged). Rather, the authors are intending to provide guidelines and explanations about particular relational experiences that tend to be corrective for specific developmental issues. Timing, context, and situational variables all need to be taken into consideration by the therapist in devising an appropriate therapeutic treatment plan.

Finally, very few patients clearly fit into one diagnostic category. Most of the patients we see manifest mixed

Table 6.1. Object Relations Therapy of Six Personality Disorders

Borderline Disorder	Schizoid	Hysteroid
Stage of Developmental Arrest:	Autistic and early symbiotic (Johnson 1985).	Practicing and rapprochement.
Treatment by Object:	Rejection, neglect, negation of child's right to be or live (Guntrip 1969).	Withdrawal of attention, support, and approval when child begins to separate and individuate (Masterson 1981).
Developmental Failure:	Lack of adequate symbiotic attachment (Johnson 1985).	Insufficient separation and individuation.
Resulting Interpersonal Stance:	Defensive withdrawal from others.	Alternation between rage and clinging.
Structural Issues:	1. Detached self that fears regressive self-fragmentation. 2. Rigidly maintained self-other differentiation.	1. Identity diffusion. 2. Lack of object constancy. 3. Vulnerability to transitory self-fragmentation or brief psychotic episodes in regressive states.
Therapeutic Goals:	*Interpersonal* 1. Protect client from gross anxiety. 2. Establish an attachment from which client can separate. *Structural* 1. Develop cohesive sense of core self that is not defensively based (Guntrip 1969). 2. Integration of part self representations (especially of affective and cognitive part self representations).	*Interpersonal* 1. Support separation. 2. Foster individuation. *Structural* 1. Resolve splitting (Kernberg 1968). 2. Develop object constancy. 3. Develop integrated sense of self. 4. Increase frustration tolerance.

	Narcissistic	Masochistic
Corrective Interpersonal Experience:	1. Therapist must be available, contactful, present, and congruent. 2. Therapist must establish a safe relationship.	1. Therapist must set appropriate limits. 2. Therapist must balance need for support and autonomy by being a secure base from which to explore. 3. Therapist must support genuine self-expression and saying no. 4. Therapist must refrain from revenge and retaliation (Wells and Glickauf-Hughes 1986).

Preneurotic Disorder	Narcissistic	Masochistic
Stage of Developmental Arrest:	Rapprochement (Johnson 1987).	On-the-way-to-object constancy (Horner 1979, Johnson 1985).
Treatment by Object:	1. Rejection of true self (Miller 1981). 2. Uses child as selfobject or ideal object. 3. Provides admiration rather than love and acceptance.	1. Scapegoating and/or parentification. 2. Abuse, neglect, and intermittent reinforcement of dependency needs. 3. Controlling (but without self-discipline). 4. Squelching the child's will (Johnson 1985).
Developmental Failure:	1. Lack of authentic, reality-based sense of self. 2. Lack of genuine self-esteem. 3. Inability to self-soothe. 4. Inability to love.	1. Failure to identify, leading to lack of transmuting internalization of caretakers' realistic and soothing capacities (Horner 1979).
Resulting Interpersonal Stance:	1. Pseudo-independent false self presentation. 2. Manipulation, idealization, and devaluation of others. 3. Relates to others as selfobjects.	1. Alternation between anxious attachment and counterdependence. 2. Overt compliance (but covert defiance). 3. Compensatory caretaking.

(continued)

Table 6.1. *(continued)*

Preneurotic Disorder	Narcissistic	Masochistic
Structural Issues:	1. Grandiose false-self structure. 2. Central ego sensitive to slights (resulting in feelings of envy, shame, and rage).	1. Lack of complete integration in self structure. 2. Lack of transmuting internalization (Horner 1979).
Therapeutic Goals:	*Interpersonal* 1. Ability to love realistically perceived whole objects. 2. Ability to be authentic with others. *Structural* 1. Develop transmuting internalization for genuine, reality-based self-soothing and self-esteem. 2. Integrate grandiose false part self representation into nuclear core.	*Interpersonal* 1. Resolve ambivalent attachment. 2. Master separation and loss. 3. Learn to genuinely depend on others. 4. Appropriate self-assertion. *Structural* 1. Develop transmuting internalization for genuine, reality-based self-soothing and self-esteem. 2. Resolve "masochistic splitting" (Meyers 1988).
Corrective Interpersonal Experience:	1. Therapist must be non-impinging, sensitive, accepting, and attuned. 2. Therapist must provide an empathic, optimally frustrating environment (Kohut 1977). 3. Therapist must support strengths and empathize with vulnerabilities (Johnson 1987).	1. Therapist must be empathic and have genuine positive regard for client. 2. Therapist must be constant, dependable, reliable, and nonreactive. 3. Therapist must acknowledge relational mistakes. 4. Therapist must be emotionally available without being possessive, controlling, or infantilizing.

Neurotic Disorder	Obsessive-Compulsive	Hysterical
Stage of Developmental Arrest:	Late separation-individuation (anal/early oedipal).	Late oedipal.
Treatment by Object:	Harsh discipline and overcontrol of child's impulses, affects, and autonomous actions.	1. Seductive behavior of opposite-sex parent. 2. Alliance of opposite-sex parent with child against same-sex parent. 3. Castration of aggressive impulses. 4. Fosters "myth of passivity" (Krohn 1978), pseudo-dependency, and helplessness.
Developmental Failure:	Insufficient sense of autonomy leading to feelings of shame and doubt (Salzman and Thaler 1981).	1. Difficulty taking initiative. 2. Guilt about sexual and aggressive impulses. 3. Confusion between sexual and affectional needs.
Resulting Interpersonal Stance:	1. Pseudo-autonomous, self-contained presentation of self. 2. Frequent power struggles (Salzman 1985).	Pseudo-dependent, seductive.
Structural Issues:	1. Stable sense of self but lack of integration of affective experience into core self. 2. Stable object constancy but proclivity to sacrifice relationships to appease harsh superego.	1. Has developed self and object constancy. 2. Low frustration tolerance and proclivity to act out conflicts.
Therapeutic Goals:	*Interpersonal* 1. Increase value of relationship (over being right or in control). 2. Increase spontaneity, affective expression, and playfulness with others (Wells et al. 1990).	*Interpersonal* 1. Develop appropriate self-assertion, initiative, and independent actions with others. 2. Learn to distinguish between sexual and dependency needs.

(continued)

Table 6.1. (continued)

Neurotic Disorder	Obsessive-Compulsive	Hysterical
Therapeutic Goals (*continued*):	*Structural* 1. Further individuation: develop genuine sense of autonomy rather than reactivity and power struggles. 2. Soften harsh superego.	*Structural* 1. Further integration of (a) cognitive with affective self and (b) sexual and affectional self representations. 2. Increase frustration tolerance and ability to reflect rather than act out.
Corrective Interpersonal Experience:	1. Therapist must be warm, spontaneous, and emotionally expressive. 2. Therapist must model appropriate risk-taking (Wells et al. 1990). 3. Therapist must admit mistakes and let clients off the hook when they make mistakes. 4. Therapist must be nondirective and nonauthoritarian.	1. Therapist must be warm and nondirective. 2. Therapist must not dominate, get seduced, or foster too much dependency (Mueller and Aniskiewicz 1986). 3. Therapist must support strength, competence, and appropriate assertion. 4. Therapist must clarify emotions and ask for factual details.

personality or characterological issues. Furthermore, characterological issues are viewed as similar in nature to colors on a palette. Everyone has more of some and less of others. For example, a patient might have a strong masochistic component, some underlying narcissistic issues, and a tendency to use obsessive defenses under stress. However, the patient doesn't have schizoid features, has few hysterical qualities (e.g., pseudoemotionality, global perceptions, dramatic presentation), has reasonably developed object constancy, and, thus, infrequently uses splitting as a defense. The therapeutic approach prescribed for such a patient is whatever complicated mix of experiences his or her character requires (e.g., empathy, non-reactivity, insight into use of obsessive defenses, etc.).

The suggested task is neither simple nor easy. This is particularly true as many patients present in therapy with contradictory issues. For example, patients with strong narcissistic and schizoid issues require the therapist to manage the difficult balancing act of being engaged without being experienced as intrusive or engulfing. Therapists often find such patients most challenging and frequently respond to them by interpreting their conflicting needs (e.g., "When I speak, you feel invaded and when I'm quiet you feel abandoned").

While specific corrective behaviors are thus suggested in this book, we not intend to be overly categorical in understanding patient issues or to suggest that clinicians follow a simple, step-by-step treatment approach. Rather, the suggested guidelines are intended to inspire a new way for therapists to creatively use developmental theory in the treatment of their patients.

CASE EXAMPLES OF MODEL

Understanding the patient's underlying structural and developmental issues is extremely important with regard to both formulating appropriate treatment goals and ascertaining for each patient what constitutes a corrective interpersonal experience. For example, consider the ramifications of misdiagnosing a schizoid-like borderline client who employs many obsessive defenses as an obsessive-compulsive neurotic. Such a neurotic client maintains the ego strength to manifest a cohesive and integrated sense of self under stress and intense affect but presents a personality style that is overconstricted and counterdependent. In this case example, the consequence of such a misdiagnosis was that the therapist explored and encouraged the activation and expression of the client's feelings (including anger) and dependency or relationship needs. When the therapist then went on a two-week vacation, the client decompensated (e.g., had panic attacks, suicidal ideations, transient psychotic symptoms) and abruptly left the therapeutic relationship out of fear of destruction by the therapist and rage over feeling invited to depend and then rejected by the leaving.

Had the therapist recognized that the client's obsessive-compulsive defenses and cognitive style masked a borderline ego organization she would have avoided encouraging the expression of the client's underlying feelings (e.g. rage) until he had established a relatively stable and positive relationship with the therapist and been able to use that relationship to augment self-soothing and self-validating functions. In addition the therapist would have focused on the client's tenuous capacity for object constancy rather than on the expression of his dependency needs per se. As a result of this change in focus, the therapist could have helped the client to better anticipate his reactions to the therapist leaving on vacation and could have joined the client in creating strategies for managing his internal turmoil/separation anxieties during the therapist's absence.

The following cases illustrate different types of corrective interpersonal experiences that are needed by patients who have different developmental deficits and who repeatedly express the wish to leave therapy mid-session. In the case of the schizoid patient (who has experienced chronic rejection and neglect by objects leading to the lack of an adequate symbiotic attachment), a corrective interpersonal experience requires, above all, that the therapist "be there" (Johnson 1985, p. 83). The schizoid must first be helped to establish an attachment (from which he or she can later separate). The therapist facilitates this attachment by being contactful, present, and congruent. Thus, should a schizoid patient request to leave mid-session, the appropriate therapeutic response would be to encourage the patient to remain and to process the wish to leave the session early with him or her. We have observed that schizoid patients often make this request as a means of testing their assumption that they are not wanted.

In contrast to the literal abandonment often experienced by schizoid patients, narcissistic patients have experienced the physical presence of, but insufficient attunement from, the selfobjects in their early lives. Rather than having caretakers who mirrored and empathized with them, they learned to accommodate themselves to parental needs, giving up their true selves to serve as their parents' ideal objects or selfobjects (Miller 1981). As a result, narcissists fail to develop an authentic, reality-based sense of self. Consequently, they greatly fear the engulfment of their own impoverished selves into the needs and demands of others.

For the narcissistic patient, a corrective interpersonal experience involves the therapist being a non-impinging, sensitive, highly attuned, "good-enough" (Winnicott 1958) selfobject who provides the narcissist with the necessary functions that were missed during early development (e.g., mirroring, echoing, admiring, soothing, empathy). Should a narcissistic patient thus express a wish to leave mid-session, the appropriate response would be to comply with the request (without interpreting it) and for therapists to warmly tell the patient that they will see him or her next week. One narcissistic patient both frequently left therapy mid-session and took a one-year leave of absence from therapy after nine months of treatment. For this patient, simply accepting his need to move away from and to return to the therapist without interpreting it or rejecting him was the most crucial element of treatment during the first phase of therapy. When this patient did return for long-term treatment, he did so with the clear sense that his motivation for doing so was internal rather than an attempt to please the therapist. At this phase in treatment, the patient's absences were interpreted. For narcissistic and borderline patients, the therapists' remaining a secure and emotionally available base as the patients move toward them and away from them to explore the environment helps patients to rework their unresolved issues from the rapprochement subphase of separation-individuation.

In summary, the strengths and weaknesses of the clinical or treatment applications of current object relations theories and interpersonal theory have been described. An alternative model of object relations therapy (including its basic premises and practical applications) has been articulated. In this model, therapy is seen as providing opportunities for a corrective interpersonal experience to help patients (a) modify their interpersonal template of self and others, (b) better master unresolved developmental issues, and (c) assume more varied and flexible interpersonal stances. The stage of developmental arrest, environmental treatment and resulting developmental failures, structural issues, and interpersonal style of six personality disorders were explored. Therapeutic goals for resolving these developmental failures, rectifying structural deficits, and modifying interpersonal style were suggested. The necessary corrective interpersonal experience for accomplishing these goals was articulated for each disorder. This experience augments the interpretive process so that patients' new understandings become more experience based. In Chapters 7 and 8, this model of treatment will be particularly applied to the preneurotic masochistic character.

7

Psychotherapy of the Masochistic Personality: Providing a Corrective Relationship

The masochistic personality described in this book is structured at the preneurotic level of ego and object relations development (Horner 1979). Like narcissistic personalities structured at this level, masochists often manifest substantial deficits in their ability to self-soothe and to regulate their self-esteem. Masochistic patients thus often need positive regard and accurate empathy to help them repair these deficits and to develop a more friendly observing ego in place of their harshly critical one. Masochists also need to understand their motivations behind such symptoms as (a) their intractable attachments to predominantly critical and rejecting love objects, (b) their overdetermined caretaking, and (c) their tendency to provoke others into becoming angry with them when they believe that they are only trying to be helpful.

In providing masochistic patients with empathy, therapists enable them to both feel known and to know themselves better. Some of the empathic statements a therapist might offer to a masochistic patient are (a) "You believe that if you could only figure out the right thing to do that she would change," (b) "Somehow, no matter what you say, what you believe most truly is that things are your fault," (c) "You feel more confident about being loved when people depend on you than when you depend on them," and (d) "When people compliment you, you think that they're conning you, whereas you believe insults."

It is important for therapists to understand why masochistic patients feel, think, and behave as they do in order to provide them with the particular type of corrective relationship that will best facilitate their efforts to work through their particular unresolved developmental issues. In treating a masochistic patient with object relations therapy, therapists are thus advised to provide the patient with a corrective interpersonal experience that will help him or her to develop a greater sense of basic trust and to become less anxiously attached to significant others. Therapists are further advised to address these patients' primary structural issues of incomplete object and self-constancy by providing masochists with opportunities to form transmuting internalizations of the therapist's realistic capacities for soothing, empathy, and genuine regard. This completion of object and self-constancy reflects a modification of the masochistic patient's mental template such that the good and the bad self and object representations are each integrated and carry a realistic and predominantly positive valence.

The internalization and development of self-regulatory functions can be realized only through the activation of the masochist's true self. In the early phases of treatment, the therapist thus needs to pay particular attention to the possible expression of the masochistic patient's false self or "adaptive child," which functions as an old survival mechanism and an unfortunate resistance to therapy. When the therapist senses that the working alliance with the patient is with the patient's compliant, false self, this circumstance needs to be noted along with the acknowledgment of how hard it would be to let the relationship develop without trying to earn love or avoid rejection/abandonment by meeting the other person's needs. The success of the therapy may well depend on the therapist's ability to help the masochistic patient to identify the self-defeating as well as protective nature of the false "good" self and to mobilize the patient's true self. If the patient's true self is not activated, "the work of therapy is not experienced as real and cannot be integrated or sustained" (Horner 1991, p. 238).

This chapter describes some prominent features of a corrective therapeutic experience for preneurotic masochistic patients. These features include (a) therapist dependability, (b) supporting the patient's autonomy, (c) strengthening the patient's observing ego, (d) acknowledging therapeutic errors, (e) offering sincere positive regard, (f) being realistic, (g) hearing complaints, and (h) alternating between support and confrontation. *mixed strategy*

It is important to note that therapists cannot "make" patients complete transmuting internalizations. Patients must be ready and motivated in order to avail themselves of the therapist's help. To this end, therapists will need to help the patient analyze and work through resistances as they arise. Typical resistances encountered in the treatment of masochistic patients include (a) fears of dependency, (b) avoidance of shame, (c) feeling undeserving of help, (d) confusing control or resistance with true autonomy, (e) fear of the "beast within" (especially their own anger), and (f) fear of losing the therapist by becoming healthy (e.g., autonomous selfhood). As a result of these fears, the masochistic patient may manifest a negative therapeutic transference reaction to correct interpretations or impending positive change. Further discussion of resistances will occur throughout the next two chapters.

DEPENDABILITY

As masochists were often raised in a highly unpredictable (Glickauf-Hughes and Wells 1991) and frequently abusive environment, one important aspect of a corrective relationship for masochistic patients is the therapist's constancy, dependability, and reliability. Over time, a generally dependable, predictable stance tends to counteract the paradigm of intermittent reinforcement that masochists are accustomed to experiencing. It is extremely important that therapists avoid becoming reactive with masochistic patients, particularly when they catastrophize. As masochistic patients may arouse strong feelings in therapists, experiential approaches can be dangerous unless therapists remain very aware of their own countertransference issues and reactions. For example, a masochistic patient repeatedly complaining about feeling devastated at work can elicit feelings of anxiety in the therapist, propelling the therapist to offer premature, unsolicited, and often unhelpful advice (e.g., suggesting that the patient confront his or her boss, or find a new job). In contrast, therapists are most helpful to masochists when they assume the stance of a calm, rational adult. This behavior is less important and may at times be counterindicated with other character types (e.g., obsessive-compulsives) where spontaneity, emotionality, and moderate unpredictability may be helpful (Wells et al. 1990).

A second aspect of the therapist's dependability involves assuming a position of "friendly dominance" (Leary 1957). Due to the masochists' frequent difficulty receiving from others and their propensity to assume the dominant caretaker role in their relationships, it is often important for therapists of masochistic patients to assume the care-taking role themselves in order to help reverse this tendency. For example, one patient frequently asked the therapist if she was talking too much and wearing her out.

This caretaker role often manifests in the therapist functioning as a container or auxiliary ego whenever masochists undermine themselves, lose hope, catastrophize, sabotage themselves, or get stuck in feelings of failure when the prospect of some significant advance is imminent. For example, when one patient failed one portion of his preliminary examinations and began to catastrophize that his career was ruined, the therapist calmly went over all the details with him to determine what was and wasn't a realistic concern and how he might handle the genuine problems. Masochists have received very little help of this nature from parents and other adults throughout their lives.

The therapist also needs to serve as a selfobject for the patient. This includes carefully attending to and remembering what the patient has to communicate and offering responses that indicate an attempt to understand and appreciate the patient's particular point of view. In the previous example, it was important for the therapist to first understand how frightened and ashamed the patient was and how this incident stimulated memories of traumatic failure experiences as a child before helping him gain a more objective perspective about his current situation.

It is often difficult, however, for masochists to tolerate being in a relationship where the other person assumes the friendly dominant position. Psychotherapists (as patients) who have a masochistic character frequently report how much more difficult it is for them to sit in the patient chair. Furthermore, masochistic patients often make caretaking statements to their therapist such as, "It must be hard hearing people's problems all day." At such times, it is helpful to reflect back to the masochist how uncomfortable it must be for him or her to receive help.

While masochists tend to be caretakers in relationships, they often were "pseudo-mature children" (Speers and Marter 1980) who received insufficient help in growing up. It is thus useful at times to provide them with the "management function of therapy" (Winnicott 1965). In this capacity, the therapist helps the patient to manage his or her problems in daily living, including at times giving guidance and adult information. In the previous example, the therapist helped the patient determine the nature of the problems that needed remediation and the easiest way to accomplish this. Such an approach would be counterindicated with hysterical patients who maintain a "myth of passivity" (Krohn 1978) and are usually more capable than they either behave or believe about themselves.

While it is important for the therapist to be constant and dependable, the therapist must first address masochistic patients' resistance to dependency before they are able to effectively use the therapeutic relationship for a corrective experience. Masochists can feel excessively vulnerable when they are dependent and dislike not being the one in control. In addition, they often experience caretaking, especially compliments or positive feedback, as a Trojan horse (Glickauf-Hughes and Wells 1991) and believe that if they depend upon the therapist that they will inevitably be hurt, abandoned, or humiliated. For example, one patient experienced the therapist's positive feedback as an attempt to manipulate her. It was thus important to understand how her parents had used compliments in this manner.

As a consequence of internalizing the burden of badness (Fairbairn 1943), masochists often consciously or unconsciously believe that they are not really deserving of help or that it is disloyal to the family portrait of them (e.g., as a "loser") to be part of a successful therapy. Finally, masochists can fear that the therapist (like their parents) really wishes to squelch their will and so must be resisted in order to protect autonomous selfhood. Masochists frequently confuse reactive defensiveness or resistance with true autonomy.

SUPPORTING THE PATIENT'S AUTONOMY

While it is important to be dependable with masochistic patients, it is equally important to support their autonomy. When providing the management function of therapy, it is essential that therapists resist behaving with masochistic patients in an intrusive, possessive, or rigidly controlling manner. The parents of masochists often attempted to squelch the will of their children (Johnson 1985). In response, these children become very strong willed as a means of preserving their emerging sense of self. For example, one male patient reported that as a child, his father would tell him that if he heard one more word out of his mouth, he would hit him with a belt. The patient responded to his father by saying, "One more word!"

Thus, in treating masochistic patients it is important to validate their willfulness before helping them to see what their willfulness costs them. To accomplish this task, therapists are advised to offer realistic support of the masochistic patient's disagreements with the therapist. In addition to validating the "grain of truth" or giving the patient his or her due, statements such as the following may be helpful (a) "It is important to be able to say 'no,'" (b) "You need to be able to say "no" before you can say 'yes,'" (c) "It's all right to have a mind of your own," and

(d) "Your strong will helped you to survive as a child." After the masochistic patient's willfulness has been sufficiently validated, the therapist can then help the masochist to understand the negative consequences of his or her stubbornly willful behavior (e.g., power struggles, self-sabotaging behavior). For example, one masochistic patient needed to feel understood in regard to his need to control the session (i.e., that filibustering was the only way to get heard in his family). However, it was also important for him to eventually become aware that this behavior prevented him from getting a connection with the therapist and being helped.

Another component of supporting the autonomy of the masochistic patient involves accepting the masochist's libidinal ego or childlike qualities without subtly infantilizing him or her. Masochists frequently present themselves as being in a state of crisis. Therapists of masochistic patients may thus feel a strong countertransference pull to rescue them. It is, however, more useful to these patients for their therapists to allow them to both make and learn from their own mistakes. For example, one masochistic patient in group psychotherapy had a history of having relationships with extremely rejecting men. She was currently infatuated with a new man who both had another partner and did not reciprocate her romantic interest. The man needed a new roommate and invited her to move in with him. She felt enthusiastic about this possibility and asked the therapy group for their advice.

Historically, when this patient brought problems of this nature to the group, group members would confront her and warn her against taking the action that she was considering and she would respond to this confrontation with either openly rebellious or more covert, passive-resistive noncompliance. On this occasion, the group therapists suggested to the group that it might be more useful to the patient to help her sort out this complicated problem for herself. To facilitate this process, the group therapists asked the patient what she thought the advantages and disadvantages of this decision were and asked her if she had any "red flags" about it. The latter question can be especially helpful as a means of encouraging masochistic patients to pay attention to their intuitions about people and situations that cause them discomfort. It is often useful for masochists to entertain the perspective that they can learn from each decision and with new information can remake decisions accordingly.

STRENGTHEN THE PATIENT'S OBSERVING EGO

One very important aspect of facilitating masochistic patients' sense of autonomy is to help them improve their reality testing and strengthen their observing ego. This can be facilitated by the therapist serving as an auxiliary ego for these patients when they become overwhelmed and catastrophize. It is also useful to masochists for therapists to help them see their realistic alternatives in difficult situations. For example, patients who are in self-defeating, problematic relationships can be shown that their only alternatives are not being a martyr or leaving their partner.

Another means of improving masochistic patients' ability to reality test is to objectively examine with them (step by step and detail by detail) how their interpersonal problems develop. Thus, when one patient came to the therapy session and said that her marriage was awful and that no one would ever love her, the therapist responded by asking her to tell her from the beginning what happened that week with her husband. Masochists tend toward catastrophizing and categorizing (especially making judgment about who is to blame) in assessing their interpersonal problems. They experience problems with others as erupting out of nowhere and they tend to attribute these problems to their own "badness" or, occasionally, the other's "meanness." Neither explanation is satisfying or helpful to them in averting future difficulties. It is important in working with masochistic patients to help them learn to nonjudgmentally examine each party's contributions to relationship problems. Over time, the patient begins to internalize this approach and to better understand his or her interpersonal difficulties without experiencing diminished self-esteem.

Masochists' reality testing can be further improved by the therapist's validation of the truth in the patient's perceptions. Thus, in the last example, the therapist said to the patient, "I can understand why you felt hurt when he forgot your birthday and how you ended up feeling blamed when he said you were too demanding." Nothing is more strengthening to one's sense of self and self-esteem than being able to rely upon one's own intuitions. As relationships are so important to masochists, when others are hurtful to them they tend to deny their perceptions and to rationalize and deny their significant other's behavior. It is thus important to help the masochistic patient see that if a choice must be made between trusting their own perceptions and trusting other people, they are ultimately better off if they trust themselves. Eventually learning how to empathize with others during disputes while still empathizing with oneself can also be of great help to the masochist.

ACKNOWLEDGE THERAPEUTIC ERRORS

It is important that the therapist be able to acknowledge his or her own mistakes with a masochistic patient when they occur (Smaldino 1984). Masochists have been blamed their entire lives by both parents and partners and have come to believe that relational difficulties are all their fault. When they become angry at the therapist, it is thus necessary for reparation of their self-esteem that the therapist be able to openly examine the aspects of the masochist's accusations that are valid and to be able to admit to making mistakes without being self-effacing. For example, the therapist said to one patient (who felt criticized by the therapist): "I can understand how that could have sounded critical to you, although I hadn't intended it that way."

It is not recommended that therapists be insincere or untruthful with masochistic patients. Rather, it is suggested that there is usually some aspect of truth to people's perceptions and that it is important for that truth to be acknowledged. The therapist's acknowledgment of his or her relational mistakes is very reparative for masochists as it helps them both to trust their perceptions more and to believe to a greater extent that everything isn't always their fault. The therapist's acknowledgment of honest mistakes also increases the masochists' trust that the therapist will not blame them or make them feel crazy.

SINCERE POSITIVE REGARD

An essential component of a corrective therapeutic relationship for masochistic patients is that the therapist genuinely like them. While most people want to be liked, this need is far more important for masochists than it is for many other patients (e.g., obsessive-compulsives). Historically, masochists have experienced parental disregard ranging from lack of interest to contempt. For example, one masochistic patient was told by his father, "I love you because you're my son but I don't like you." This lack of regard by parents was often attributed to the child's qualities (e.g., excessive demandingness) rather than parental limitations (e.g., extreme self-preoccupation). Furthermore, when masochists do feel valued it is often for what they do for others rather than for who they are.

Thus, if the therapist does not find a particular masochistic patient to be genuinely likable, it is recommended that the therapist refer the patient to another clinician. Otherwise, masochists, who are highly sensitive to inauthenticity, are likely to experience the therapeutic relationship as a realistic repetition of their family's hypocrisy. It must be noted, however, that even when the therapist does have genuine positive regard for the masochistic patient, the patient will still not initially believe it. In the latter case, however, the patient's feelings can more clearly be treated as a transference phenomenon.

BEING REALISTIC

It is important in the treatment of masochistic patients that the therapist be realistic with them. As a means of coping with a difficult and often abusive childhood, masochists frequently utilized fantasy. In addition, many masochistic patients have been reared reading fairy tales, and many fairy tales have a masochistic theme (e.g., Beauty and the Beast). Masochists thus often entertain many illusions about life. They have a tendency to both want too much from relationships and to settle for too little. They thus need the therapist's help in understanding what is realistic to expect from others (e.g., "You may not be able to expect your partner to read your mind but you ought to be able to count on spending more than one night each week with him or her").

As part of this process, it is important that the therapist not promise masochistic patients more than they are realistically able to give them, thereby establishing a narcissistic collusion. It is a common countertransference error in psychotherapy with the masochistic personality for the therapists to try to be an all-good object for their masochistic patients in order to make reparation to them for their extremely difficult life circumstances. Such implicit contracts are impossible to fulfill and are therefore ultimately disappointing to patients.

In contrast, it is helpful to teach masochists about the "seventy percent rule" (Wells and Glickauf-Hughes 1986), which states that one cannot realistically expect another human being to be available and understanding more than seventy percent of the time, but one does not need to accept much less. The seventy percent rule is also a good guideline for therapists of masochists to use for themselves with their masochistic patients.

LISTENING TO COMPLAINTS

In the early stages of treatment, the therapist must spend a great deal of time listening to and empathizing with the masochist's complaints about myriad forms of mistreatment by the world. It is particularly important to understand their chronic complaints that "therapy isn't helping." For example, one masochistic patient asked the therapist how he could be expected to believe that she could help him when she couldn't even get her clock repaired.

When masochists complain about the therapist, it is useful to interpret their underlying belief that no one can help them and to facilitate their understanding that they are experiencing a very old feeling or even a feeling memory. The therapist might then note that he or she has never thought of the patient as unhelpable although it is clear that the patient sometimes sees him- or herself that way. Finally, it is important to help masochistic patients avoid getting stuck in complaining but to eventually learn to get what they need and want from other people.

ALTERNATING BETWEEN SUPPORT AND CONFRONTATION

For optimal growth masochistic patients need an individually tailored balance between the therapist's warmth and understanding and the therapist's judicious use of caring confrontation. Group therapy can be helpful as patients are able to get both types of feedback from different persons.

In general, masochistic patients need an initial period of support in order to help them to develop sufficient trust in the therapist to enable them to tolerate the therapist's eventual confrontation of their provocative and passive-aggressive behaviors. Masochists often behave in a subtly provocative manner that often induces sadistic and aggressive responses in others. Eventually, they may behave this way with the therapist as well. Prior to therapy, masochistic patients generally have very little awareness that they engage in this process and don't have much understanding of how and why they do this. For example, a third grade teacher could not understand why the principal of her school was angry at her so often when she was trying her very best to discipline her students as the principal requested. She said it wasn't her fault that one of her students threw clay at the principal when he came to her class to observe. This teacher was unaware of how she subtly reinforced her students for acting out her own anger toward authority figures.

When sufficient trust is established in the therapeutic relationship and the therapist notices that he or she is beginning to have aggressive feelings and fantasies toward the patient, the therapist may now begin to process these reactions with the patient. Masochists must learn how they frustrate other people (i.e., their exact behaviors) and why they frustrate them.

One way in which masochists frustrate others may be through the use of projective identification. Because masochists are afraid of their anger, they may defend themselves by projecting their own angry self representations onto others and then behaving in such a way as to induce anger in the other. The masochist can then feel more justified in expressing anger in reaction to the other's hostility. For example, one masochistic patient tended to speak in a whiny voice whenever she was angry at the therapist. Masochists who grew up with negative intimacy may also annoy others as a way of inducing a familiar connection with them. Finally, as masochists are often rigidly defended and as pain can be more impelling than pleasure, sometimes masochists only respond to negative stimuli. For example, one group member discounted comments from supportive group members and only responded to group members who were angry and critical of her.

Because of the masochistic patients' rigid defenses, at times confrontation is the only feedback that they notice and to which they respond. Ultimately, however, the therapist must help masochists to become aware of and fully experience gentleness and love from other people and to make it part of their lives.

To conclude, in large measure a corrective relationship is designed to help the preneurotic masochist repair
structural deficits by helping the patient to develop and
stabilize transmuting internalizations of (a) self-accept-
ance and self-soothing (through empathy, validation, nor-
malizing, and perspective); (b) self-esteem (through
empathy, recognition, and appreciation of realistic at-
tributes and strivings); (c) internal security operations
(through nonreactive regard in crises and confident exploration of the patient's evolving abilities to work through
problems); and (d) self-activation (through curiosity and
interest in the patient's real self and assuming a nondirec-
tive stance). As masochists integrate transmuting internalizations of the therapist's warm explorations, gentle
confrontations, and adult perspective into their central
ego, they become better able to self-regulate and thus
function more independently. In the early phases of treatment, therapists are reminded to attend to the activation of
the masochist's true self since the success of the therapy
and the aforementioned internalization process depends
upon it.

8

Psychotherapy of the Masochistic Personality: Central Treatment Issues and Goals

The therapist of masochistic patients helps them to further their capacity for basic trust and for resolving anxious attachments by being a nonreactive, dependable, realistic, sincerely caring individual who strengthens their ego and supports their autonomy. The therapist alternates between listening patiently to patients' problems and confronting their subtly provocative behavior. In the process of providing a corrective relationship, therapists will need to help these patients to (a) master feelings of separation and loss; (b) set appropriate limits: (c) express anger more appropriately; (d) learn to be "streetwise"; (e) learn to distinguish between love and longing; (f) become more aware of and able to appropriately express dependency needs; (g) learn to choose loving, giving, dependable significant others; and (h) develop more stable self-esteem. This chapter discusses in some detail how therapists can help masochistic patients achieve each of these goals.

HELPING PATIENTS MASTER FEELINGS OF
SEPARATION AND LOSS

As previously discussed, loss and separation present difficult problems for the masochistic personality and account for a number of their symptoms (e.g., remaining in difficult relationships). Helping masochists deal more effectively with separation and loss is thus a crucial component of treatment.

There are several therapeutic strategies that are specifically designed to help masochistic patients to gain mastery over their difficulties with separation and loss. The first strategy is to help them to internalize the therapist as a good-enough, comforting object. This includes having tolerable separations and being as responsive as possible to their needs. It is often helpful to see masochistic patients more often than one time per week. However, in doing so, it is better to meet on a regular basis rather than to frequently provide extra appointments in response to crises. Overresponding to crises can reinforce their perception that they are most loved when suffering or ill.

Although the masochist's difficulties with separations are not nearly at the level of severity as that of the borderline patient, strategies used for helping borderlines to establish object constancy (Wells and Glickauf-Hughes 1986) can also be useful in working with masochistic patients. Included among these are the use of transitional objects and journals during the therapist's vacations. In the case of the latter, when patients are feeling alone, depressed, and frightened during the therapist's absence they are initially encouraged to write in a journal letters to the therapist describing their thoughts or feelings. Whenever possible, the patient is encouraged to write an educated guess as to how the therapist would be likely to respond. Eventually, most patients begin to write to them selves and to integrate the therapist's responses into their own thinking. The journal can thus serve as a helpful tool in the establishment and solidification of transmuting internalizations.

Another important component in the process of masochistic patients' developing transmuting internalizations of therapist responses is the internalization of therapist attitudes. More important at times than the verbal message that therapists offer patients are their nonverbal or implied messages. By responding in a calm, nonreactive manner to masochists' frequent crises, therapists offer masochistic patients the opportunity to internalize a sense of confidence in dealing with their problems. The therapist's warmth is likewise internalized into self-regard, including the belief that he or she is a lovable person. The therapist's patience can help patients to become less fearful of the world and more patient with themselves. Finally, the therapist's authenticity and acceptance help masochists feel more accepting of their real selves. An authentic connection can be a curative factor for individuals struggling with the problem of anxious attachment (John Nardo, personal communication, 1989).

While retaining good limits for themselves, therapists need to allow masochistic patients to both move toward and away from the therapist as much as possible. Masochists have often incompletely resolved the rapprochement subphase (Mahler et al. 1975) of separation-individuation. It is thus helpful to understand and accept the masochistic patient's periodic needs to cling to and separate from the therapist. In particular, it is important to support masochistic patients in their desire to take a leave of absence from therapy (without interpreting it) should they request one (Horner 1979). For both masochistic and narcissistic patients, this approach is trust building and self-affirming. Allowing these patients to leave therapy without losing the

emotional connection with the therapist can be enor-
mously helpful to them in their resolution of the separation-
individuation process as it helps them to separate with a
sense of a secure base that they can return to. When
appropriate, a minimal interpretation that can serve both
to facilitate an understanding of the leaving and yet keep
the door open is sometimes useful: "Sometimes when
people enter therapy when they really need it because of a
crisis, they leave therapy when they don't need it any-
more. Later they may come back because they want to"
(John Nardo, personal communication, 1990).

Finally, while it is neither possible nor desirable for
the therapist to always be available at the patient's time of
great need, it is important that early in therapy masochistic patients know how to reach the therapist (or a supportive friend) when they are still unable to self-soothe.
This is particularly important as these patients learn to set
limits with their partners, since their partners may initially
protest these limits by responding with punishing withdrawal. Masochists must learn that there is not only one
mother but rather that the world is rich with people upon
whom they can depend.

HELPING PATIENTS LEARN TO SET
APPROPRIATE LIMITS

Due to the potentially negative interpersonal repercus-
sions of helping masochists learn to set better limits with
significant others, it is often important to first help them to
master loss and separation before beginning this process.
Once masochists have gained better mastery over the
experiences of separation and loss, they are less fearful of
being abandoned or unloved as a result of saying no to

people. The therapist can then begin to help patients learn to set better limits for themselves by using both the processes of teaching and modeling.

In the former process, the patient presents the therapist with an example of how he or she is having difficulty. For example, one masochistic patient complained about a friend who would phone her late at night and continue to call until she answered the phone. The therapist recommended to the patient that she tell her friend that while she enjoys talking to her on the phone, she needs to get up early in the morning for work and she would like her to call before ten o'clock. The therapist further encouraged the patient to turn her phone machine on after ten o'clock at night. In teaching masochists to set limits, it is important to help them anticipate potential angry responses from the individuals in their life who are receiving limits from them for the first time. Therapists may recommend to their masochistic patients that they listen to and empathize with their friends' and partner's nonabusive expression of anger regarding the limit. In the previous example, the therapist suggested to the patient that she empathize with her friend's frustration about not being able to reach her when she wants to before telling her friend again firmly but kindly that she really needs her sleep.

The second and perhaps more important method of helping masochists learn to set appropriate limits is by the therapist modeling how to set limits when his or her limits are pushed by the masochistic patient. For example, although the therapist had a twenty-four hour cancellation policy, one masochistic patient frequently canceled her appointment only a few hours prior to her appointment (and then requested that she not be charged for the appointment). This patient was a special-education teacher who reported canceling her appointment because of a crisis in which one of her students needed her. The therapist commented that it seemed as though the patient believed that both she and the therapist shouldn't have any limits. The therapist firmly maintained her twenty-four hour cancellation policy (explaining why it was necessary) but empathized with the patient's frustration about this limit. Through the process of modeling, it is hoped that the masochistic patient begins to identify with the process of setting and maintaining loving but firm limits in one's life.

It is important at times to help masochists learn to limit other people's abusive behavior toward them as well as learning to limit the amount of caretaking that they do. Masochistic patients have little understanding regarding acceptable boundaries in the expression of anger. They tend to alternate between cutting off their partner's appropriate expression of anger and tolerating rage reactions. A helpful guideline for masochistic patients is to encourage them to listen to other people's expressions of angry feelings about their behaviors but not to tolerate blaming, contempt, screaming, or any form of physical violence.

Finally, setting appropriate limits is generally very difficult for masochists to do. A large part of the therapeutic work in this area thus involves processing their resistance. Some of the fears that masochists have about setting limits involve (a) not being loved, (b) not feeling like a good person, and (c) being abandoned. It is important for the therapist to help the masochistic patient begin to distinguish between the real versus transferential nature of these concerns. In addition, masochists can also secretly, if not overtly, feel proud of their ability to tolerate and cope with a wide range of abnormal or atypical behaviors. Helping masochists appreciate the price that they pay for this investment in tolerance as well as educating these patients to the benefits of learning to set one's own good limits may help these patients work through their resistances.

HELPING PATIENTS LEARN TO EXPRESS ANGER APPROPRIATELY

In addition to setting limits on other people's inappropriate expression of anger, it is important to help masochistic patients to learn to identify and appropriately express their own angry feelings. As anger is an ego-dystonic experience for masochists, the first step in helping them learn to express anger is to help them learn to recognize and accept it. Masochists are very afraid of their angry feelings as they anticipate their anger leading to separation and loss (Menaker 1953). Furthermore, as masochists have often been shamed by parents for expression of anger, anger is associated with their "bad" self. The therapist can first help masochistic patients to recognize anger by empathizing with what they must have been feeling in difficult situations (or in instances where the patient behaved passive-aggressively). Furthermore, when empathizing with the masochist's anger, it is best to begin by using moderate and tentative suggestions: "If I were you, I might have felt irritated with her when she said that" or "I can see how you could have felt annoyed with how intrusive your mother was with you sometimes." This style of presentation helps the masochist more comfortably identify with and accept aggressive possibilities.

As masochistic patients become more aware of their angry feelings, it is helpful to teach them how to express these feelings without either presenting as passive-aggressive or losing their temper. Masochists need to learn how to express anger without blaming, placating, or losing their observing ego. Some helpful guidelines are (a) making short, simple nonaccusatory statements about their feelings, (b) learning to observe and respond to distracting and escalating tactics made by the person with whom they are angry (e.g., changing the subject, blaming back, screaming, and withdrawing), (c) being proactive rather than reactive, and (d) taking "time-outs" from the fight if either party begins to lose their temper. It is often helpful for masochists to have guidelines about what to say to the other during a fight such as (a) "I understand that you're also angry about Y but right now I'm angry about X and I'd like you to hear my anger first. Later on I'll listen to you" and (b) "This fight seems to be getting out of control and I'm afraid that we're going to begin saying things that will hurt one another. Let's take some time to both cool off and get back together in a half hour to talk again." As mentioned previously, it often helps masochistic patients for the therapist to listen to detailed reports of their fights in order to increase their reality testing and develop non-defensive strategies.

Teaching masochistic patients to appropriately express their anger is an extremely important alternative to their leaving a difficult relationship or remaining but feeling like a martyr. It is helpful to explain to the masochistic patient that anger does not need to lead to a chronic state of tension as it did in their families. Instead, anger can be used as an important signal that indicates that something is wrong. Anger can also help provide these patients with information about what is important to them or about where their limits actually are. Furthermore, when appropriately expressed, anger can help clear the air and restore intimacy in a relationship.

HELPING PATIENTS LEARN TO BE "STREETWISE"

In addition to learning to use anger as a signal, masochistic patients also need to learn to attend to and trust their perceptions of events that may signify potential problems. As children, masochists frequently used massive denial as a defense. As a result, they have tendencies to alternate between being naive and paranoid. So much was problematic in their families of origin that they learned to cope by minimizing, denying, or rationalizing relevant danger signals. They continue to do this as adults, particularly with significant others. For example, one masochistic patient (whose wife left him) recalled his wife telling him shortly after they met that she had left every man with whom she had ever been involved.

It is helpful to teach masochists to pay greater attention to these types of "red flags" and to learn to identify subtle contempt and "dangerous" people. For example, one masochistic patient noted that every time she and her partner became close, he then became rejecting. The first time that this happened, he explained to her that he didn't feel well. The second time he blamed her, and the third time he questioned whether they were appropriate for each other. As masochists have a tendency to rationalize their partner's behavior, it is helpful to teach them the axiom: "The first time something occurs, it's an accident. The second time, it's a coincidence. The third time, it's a pattern."

Finally, an important aspect of helping masochistic patients learn to be more "streetwise" is to help them be able to sort out "red flags" from transference reactions. For example, one masochistic patient who experienced profound rejection by parents responded to his introverted partner as though she were trying to hurt him rather than as simply being a person who enjoyed a lot of time to herself. As masochistic patients become better able to identify and understand danger signals in the world and to sort out signals of real danger from transference reactions, there is less likelihood of their being tricked by a Trojan

horse. This trust in one's own perceptions eventually leads
to both greater self-confidence and more realistic trust in
other people.

HELPING PATIENTS LEARN TO DISTINGUISH
BETWEEN LOVE AND LONGING

Due to their experiences of both early gratification and
deprivation, masochists, like Romeo and Juliet, experience love as an impossible separation from an idealized
object (Smirnoff 1969). An old Spanish expression that
translates into "hunger is the best sauce" applies to the
inner experience of the masochistic patient. Masochists are
drawn to exciting and rejecting objects that give them the
familiar experience of relatively short bursts of intense
gratification that alternate with long periods of yearning.

Masochistic patients repeatedly report finding emotionally available, mature, consistent, loving partners to be
boring and unattractive. In addition, they tend to devalue
partners who consistently want them and treat them in a
respectful manner. Masochists need help in understanding
the fact and origin of their confusing the experiences of
love and longing. They also need to learn that a genuine,
loving, intimate relationship (while not as intense as a
troubled, unpredictable relationship) need not be boring.

In accordance with the principles of object relations
therapy, the patient may best learn these principles in his
or her relationship with the therapist. The therapeutic
relationship may be the first consistent, authentic relationship that the masochist has experienced. It is thus important that therapists do not inspire longing in patients by
promising more idealized symbiosis and encouraging
more regressive dependency needs than the patient can
realistically get met either within or outside the therapy

relationship. For example, one masochistic patient reported that her last therapist told her in the beginning of treatment that she could call him any time—day or night. This inspired yearnings for a preoedipal mother that the therapist could not realistically gratify.

HELPING PATIENTS BECOME MORE AWARE OF AND ABLE TO APPROPRIATELY EXPRESS DEPENDENCY NEEDS

As discussed in Chapter 3, masochists are caretakers who are far more comfortable giving to others than receiving from them. While becoming aware of and expressing needs is an important goal for masochistic patients, it may be one that the therapist postpones addressing until later in treatment as dependency is both frightening and ego-dystonic for them. Many masochistic patients feel a great deal of shame about their dependency needs. In a therapy group (with a high proportion of masochistic patients), one member referred to himself as feeling "slimy" when he was feeling needy. This term so resonated with the feelings of other group members, that the whole group adopted this term.

The first step in helping masochistic patients with ego-dystonic dependency needs is thus to help them gain insight about why they are so frightened and ashamed of their needs and how that shame currently creates their own loneliness. Most masochistic patients both desperately wish to depend upon someone and fear that their needs will overwhelm or disgust others. It is often useful to help them realize that this fear is most likely a feeling memory of childhood. Such a memory reflects an earlier time when their needs really were too much for their inadequate parents who expressed disapproval nonverbally as well as verbally.

It is important to help masochistic patients understand that the reason they do feel so needy at times has
more to do with inadequately getting their needs met in the
world (due to their difficulty receiving and proclivity toward caretaking) than with some innate unlovability. It is
useful to instruct them that when they get and metabolize
"three square meals" a day, they will not feel so hungry.

The second step in helping masochistic patients become more aware of their needs is thus educational. For
example, many masochistic patients use the word *needy*
as a generic term since they have little understanding of
what it is that they need. In childhood, their parents were
generally so unattuned with them that masochists never
learned to make associations between comforting behaviors from others and the internal experience of being
soothed. It is thus helpful to teach these patients about the
things that most people need (e.g. love, attention, affection,
understanding). It may also be useful to help them understand their proclivity to project their own needs onto
others. For example, when they need a hug, they might
offer one. Becoming aware of this process may provide
them with further cues about their own needs.

A final way that therapists may help masochistic
patients gain greater identification with and acceptance of
their dependency needs is for therapists to model talking
about needs. Through this process, the patient may further
come to see needs as a respectable, normal part of human
existence as well as to begin to learn appropriate means of
expression. For example, the therapists may plant a seed
or normalize needs for a masochistic patient in denial by
noting that the therapist is aware that if he or she were in
the patient's place, he or she would probably want reassurance too.

Once masochistic patients develop a greater awareness and acceptance of their needs, the next therapeutic

task is to help them learn to express their needs in a manner that optimizes the opportunity for them being gratified by others. Masochists have a tendency to express needs indirectly, vicariously, and with a subtle negativism (anger, resentment, discouragement) that reflects their underlying belief that their needs will not be met (e.g., "You probably don't want to go to the movies with me tonight"). This problem is further compounded by their propensity to feel most comfortable showing their needs and attempting to get them met with people who are generally depriving, unresponsive, or unreliable.

It is helpful to teach masochistic patients how they unconsciously sabotage getting their needs met as well as teaching more effective alternatives. For example, one masochistic patient had a propensity to whine when she was feeling needy. Her whining was a reflection of both her feelings of frustrated need and her sense of futility about ever being gratified. This patient eventually came to understand that when she heard herself whining, it usually meant she was feeling both needy and angry about being ungratified. She learned that when she became aware of this, if she approached a friend and said, "I feel down today. Can I have a hug?" or "I had a rotten day. Would you listen for a few minutes?" that she had a much better chance of being comforted by others than she did by whining. Therapy groups can provide an excellent format for masochistic patients in the process of learning to express their needs more appropriately.

HELPING PATIENTS LEARN TO CHOOSE LOVING, GIVING, DEPENDABLE SIGNIFICANT OTHERS

After masochistic patients have developed a greater understanding of their needs, it is important to help them learn to make healthier choices about where and with whom to best get their needs met. As discussed in an earlier chapter, through repetition compulsion masochists often manifest a relationship pattern in which they continue to try to get love and approval from predominantly critical and rejecting, but often romantic, intense, and idealized objects. It is important to help masochists become aware of both the presence and the futility of this particular pattern.

It is also important to help masochistic patients learn to be better observers. The people in one's life provide a great deal of information about themselves if one pays attention to it. It is important to help masochistic patients develop a healthy suspicion about "chemistry" in relationships and its tendency to make people less skilled observers. This healthy caution is especially relevant for those individuals who feel compelled to find instant intimacy. If these patients learn to proceed more slowly in romantic relationships so that they know who it is that they love, there is less probability of their being tricked by a Trojan horse and thus repeating old painful relationship patterns.

Finally, while it is important for masochistic patients to learn not to choose predominantly critical and rejecting partners, it is equally important for them to learn to appreciate loving, available partners. Like Groucho Marx, masochists often don't want to belong to any club that would have them as members. Several masochistic female patients mentioned in therapy, after seeing the film *Crossing Delancey,* that they preferred the severely narcissistic author over the loving pickle merchant.

The third aspect of learning to choose "healthy" partners thus involves helping patients to grieve their narcissistic fantasies about finding an ideal partner. Masochists often attempt to repair an old self-esteem injury by getting the approval of and merging with an idealized object. They need to learn that what will help them more is to feel loved and accepted by a kind and giving (although ordinary) human being.

HELPING PATIENTS DEVELOP MORE RESILIENT SELF-ESTEEM

One important means of helping masochistic patients to make less narcissistic object choices is by helping them to increase and stabilize their own self-esteem. As postulated by Kohut (1977) and empirically demonstrated by Rogers (1965), an effective means of accomplishing this goal is through the use of empathic understanding. Over time as masochistic patients acquire transmuting internalizations of certain realistic functions of the therapist (e.g., empathy, soothing), object constancy is completed and self-esteem becomes more stable.

A second means of helping masochistic patients increase self-esteem is to help them to develop a more realistic ego ideal. It is important for the masochist to develop an interest in dreams that are accomplishable as their tendency is to set either unrealistically high goals that they fail to meet or to sell themselves short. An important aspect of this process is supporting the masochistic patient in accomplishing his or her own goals and ideals rather than attaining them vicariously through a partner. In so doing, masochists have less narcissistic needs that they try to get met through their choice of partner.

During the course of treatment, the therapist is advised to point out the patient's tendencies to automatically minimize good feelings such as satisfaction or pride while accentuating bad feelings. Therapists need to help masochistic patients recognize their propensity to invoke or dwell on failure (real or anticipated) in the therapeutic relationship when it is predominantly benevolent and progressive or when on the verge of some significant therapeutic movement. Such chronic selective attention interferes with the goal of increasing the patient's self-esteem.

We have probed several important goals that therapists are advised to consider in treating masochistic patients in long-term psychotherapy. In accomplishing these goals, therapists help masochistic patients reduce their frequency of self-defeating behavior, allowing them to pursue the avenues of love, work, and play in a more satisfying manner.

9

Countertransference Issues

Masochistic patients have a number of personal strengths that often make them excellent candidates for psychotherapy. For example, their relational orientation facilitates their ability to bond with the therapist and develop a working alliance. Their propensity to internalize often accompanies an ability to introspect and self-reflect. Their ability to tolerate frustration allows them to endure the slow and difficult process of change that therapy involves, including therapeutic abstinence. Despite these considerable strengths, masochists can at times be difficult patients with whom to work.

This chapter explicates the type of countertransference issues that therapists are most likely to face in treating masochistic patients. Forewarning therapists about these potential pitfalls may help them to avert an impasse or to constructively manage typical countertransference feelings as they arise. These pitfalls include (a)

internalizing the masochist's suffering, (b) difficulty tolerating the masochist's refusal to receive help, (c) the desire
to provide reparation for previous injury, (d) masochistic
triangulation, (e) persecutory fantasies or behavior, and (f)
feeling grateful due to ingratiating projective identifications.

INTERNALIZING THE MASOCHIST'S SUFFERING

By definition, masochists are patients who tend to experience a great deal of suffering. They often remain in difficult
relationships long past the point that others would have
disengaged or cut their losses. Since masochists tend to
internalize the burden of badness (Fairbairn 1943), they
also tend to blame themselves for the problematic aspects
of these situations. As a result of these proclivities, they
have a propensity to struggle with mild to severe depression.

When the therapist empathizes with masochistic patients in order to understand how the world appears from
their perspective, the therapist may thus dip into his or her
own wellspring of depression. If the therapist overidentifies
with the client, the therapist's empathy can extend past a
temporary regression in service of the ego. The therapist
may consequently experience the patient's affects directly
and in full measure, thus losing the required measure of
emotional separateness to maintain therapeutic objectivity
and preserve clear boundaries. Overidentification is a particular hazard whenever therapists, themselves, manifest
masochistic tendencies, and many therapists do (Grief
1985).

One indication that therapists may be overidentifying

with their masochistic patients is manifested in the therapist's urgency to "fix" their patients in order to diminish
the painful affects that both the patient and the therapist
are now experiencing. This sense of urgency can lead
therapists to give premature advice and then become
frustrated when their patients do not follow it. Grotnick
(1982) noted that in treating intensely suffering patients,
"when the therapist, as a result of his worry, gave in to the
patient's demands for both medication and advice, the
patient's symptoms became more severe" (p. 487). Grotnick believes that what the patient needs is for the therapist to tolerate his or her own feelings of suffering and
omnipotence. By the therapist containing and remaining
separate from the patient's suffering, the patient learns to
gain control over his or her own guilt and sense of omnipotence regarding his or her overresponsibility for allevi-
ating the suffering of others.

DIFFICULTY TOLERATING THE MASOCHIST'S
REFUSAL TO RECEIVE HELP

Masochistic patients have great difficulty receiving from
others. This more pervasive problem extends to receiving
help from the therapist. In addition, masochists tend to be
extremely ambivalent about dependency—both wishing
for and fearing it. While they desperately want help with
their life, masochists fear that if they need the therapist too
much, the therapist will betray them as previous significant others have done. Furthermore, they experience receiving help from others as a threat to their precariously
experienced sense of autonomy.

As a result of this internal struggle, masochistic patients tend to present as help-rejecting complainers. While

they frequently ask for the therapist's advice, they have an even stronger need to be their own person and solve their own problems. Furthermore, therapists who are unaware of the masochistic patient's great difficulty with separation and loss may fail to understand the patient's difficulty extricating him- or herself from painful relationships and situations.

As a consequence of what appears to be the masochist's great need for, but refusal to receive, help, the therapist can end up feeling ineffective. When therapists have a number of masochistic patients in their caseload, they may even experience a crisis of faith regarding both their own competence and the ability of therapy to help people. By understanding the underlying conflicts that propel these patients' difficulties in receiving help and by anticipating slow change as the expected course of treatment, therapists can avoid or minimize personalizing the masochist's resistance and thus feel both less frustrated with these patients and less inadequate.

THE DESIRE AND/OR ATTEMPT TO BE THE "ALL-GOOD OBJECT" WHO PROVIDES REPARATION FOR A PREVIOUS TRAUMATIC INJURY

Listening to masochists' truly tragic stories of childhood as well as to their current painful difficulties often evokes empathy and genuine concern in the therapist. This concern may develop into a wish to right the previous wrongs that these patients have suffered and to "fix" their current difficulties. With masochistic patients one often wonders, "What's a nice person like you doing in a place like that?" Therapists can sometimes feel a desire to actually provide "a nice place" for the masochist to reside at least during the therapeutic hour.

For example, throughout her childhood, one masochistic patient was frequently told by her father that she was stupid and ugly and that no one would ever love her. When she finally asserted herself and told her father that what he said was not true and that she could get love, he hit her and broke her nose. Despite a lifetime of her mother's narcissism and her father's abuse, this patient grew up to be a kind, loving, intelligent woman with fairly good ego strength. Not surprisingly, however, she was in a difficult marriage with a narcissistic, abusive husband who treated her as her parents did. The response provoked in the therapist was a great wish to help this patient and to be a different kind of "parent" to her—one who would never hurt or disappoint her. While the spirit behind such a wish is certainly admirable, executing it is impossible. To the extent that therapists subtly convey this desire to masochistic patients, it may inflame the patient's own wish for idealized symbiosis, which is ultimately disappointing. Furthermore, it does not help masochists to change their worldview, which alternates from being romantic to cynical. The therapist is better advised to attempt to be a "good-enough object" for the masochistic patient, which more realistically portrays what one can attain from relationships.

In addition to the normal compassion that one feels for a person who has suffered or is suffering, therapists are more likely to fall into the pattern of wishing to be an all-good object for masochistic patients if they are masochistic themselves or have had a masochistic parent and thus identify with or have more subjective countertransference with the patient. In such cases, therapists may vicariously attempt to heal themselves through healing their patient by being the kind of parent to the patient that they wished for themselves. Alternately, therapists may be attempting to heal their masochistic parent by being the kind of parent that they were unable to be as a child but sensed that their parent needed. In the latter case, the underlying wish may be for the masochistic patient (parent), once cured, to be able to finally be the kind of parent that the therapist wanted.

Thus, while it is a normal and understandable impulse to feel great concern as well as a desire to provide reparation to masochistic patients, acting on that wish is ultimately not in these patients' best interests. It is thus important for therapists to be aware of their countertransference issues with masochistic patients regarding their motives to "make things better" for the patient. This is particularly the case when therapists have had masochistic parents or have a somewhat masochistic character themselves.

MASOCHISTIC TRIANGULATION

One of the most common forms of countertransference that therapists may experience in working with masochistic patients is the phenomenon of "masochistic triangulation" described by Horner (1979). As previously discussed in Chapter 4, masochistic triangulation is manifested when masochistic patients act out an intrapsychic split between their good and bad internal objects within the context of a triangle. This acting out thus requires three people: (a) the bad, persecutory object (the partner); (b) the good, rescuing object (the therapist), and (c) the good self or victim (the masochist). The good, rescuing object has several functions in this triangle, including (a) containing the masochist's rage to protect the masochist from experiencing it (and thus becoming the bad self), and (b) validating the masochist's anger so that it feels morally justified. Having the hate expressed and externalized into the therapist, the masochist can then reexperience his or her positive, loving feelings for their partner.

Having served to contain the masochist's rage, the therapist may, at some point, feel propelled to urge the masochist to break off the relationship with his or her partner or may grow frustrated with the masochistic patient for not making any changes. The expression of either impulse can represent an important therapeutic error. In contrast, the therapist is advised to help masochists acknowledge their anger and rage and integrate these negative feelings with their loving feelings for their partner. The therapist must also help masochistic patients to see how triangles occur that really externalize a conflict that is within the patients themselves.

BECOMING THE PERSECUTOR

Even with the best of intentions, therapists who treat masochistic patients may find themselves unwittingly induced into the role of the persecutor. Leary (1957) observed that masochistic or self-effacing behavior tends to evoke a sadistic response in others. Gear and colleagues (1981) believe that passive masochistic patients "subconsciously induce the therapist to torture and abuse them" causing the therapist to feel "like a sadistic, powerful, master-parent" (pp. 202–203).

Masochistic patients can induce an angry or sadistic response from the therapist in a number of ways. By using projective identification, these patients can relocate their unconscious angry feelings and fantasies onto the therapist. This relocation may be induced in response to the patients' repeated, calmly expressed litanies of abuse at the hands of spouses, friends, and employers, and their passivity or self-sabotaging behavior in response to the abuse. Therapists may react by feeling an increasing agitation and the accompanying desire to retaliate against either the bad "objects" in these patients life or the patients themselves. Under such circumstances, the therapist may become unconsciously engaged in masochistic triangulation or may become overly confrontive in a manner that isn't helpful.

Therapists may also feel angry as a result of the masochistic patient's (a) passive-aggressive behaviors (e.g., repeatedly coming late, losing insurance forms, whining), (b) help-rejecting complaining, and (c) subtly provocative behavior. In a paper on masochistic transference, Brenner (1959) advised the analyst to avoid being "unconsciously tempted to participate with the patient in . . . sadomasochistic behavior: to become angry at the patient, to feel hopeless and defeated by him" (p. 223). "A model of behavior for the analyst to follow," Brenner suggested "is that of an understanding adult with a sulky, stubborn, provocative child. If the adult is wise and not unduly involved emotionally with the child, he is not upset or disturbed by such a child's behavior but remains calmly observant and understanding whatever may be the child's attempts to seduce and provoke him into a sadomasochistic episode" (p. 224).

Shapiro (1989) believes that the analyst who can survive the masochists' difficult "assaults" without either feeling destroyed or making subtle, hostile interpretations that leave the patient feeling destroyed can use their countertransference reactions as opportunities to enhance understanding. A therapeutic approach with this aim in mind is described in Chapter 8. The only caveat to this

approach is that therapists are advised to watch for patron-
ization, condescension, or infantilization of the patient.
The therapist always needs to emotionally recognize the
"adult" in the patient even when addressing the "child."
This is especially important in masochists who are both
particularly sensitive to condescension and yet have a
difficult time addressing it in any direct fashion.

FEELING GRATEFUL

A final form of countertransference that therapists may
experience in treating masochistic patients is that of
feeling grateful or appreciative toward the patient. Masochists are caretakers who tend to feel loved only for what they
do for others rather than for who they are. In subtle ways,
they tend to enact this role with the therapist as well.
Cashdan (1988) refers to this process as the projective
identification of ingratiation. "Individuals who employ
projective identifications of ingratiation consistently send
out messages regarding how much they put themselves
out for others. They notify those about them how much
they give of themselves and how unappreciated they feel"
(p. 115). Cashdan believes that projective identifications of
ingratiation are expressed in therapy through attempts on
the patient's part to be helpful and accommodating (e.g.,
making referrals to the therapist, cleaning the group room,
being very accommodating about changed appointment
times, acting as the co-therapist in group).

Therapists often respond to such behavior with feelings of appreciation that they have such a "good patient."
Eventually, appreciation may turn to guilt at taking advantage of such a good patient. Another related countertransference reaction in therapists whose parents are martyrs

(that is, who expect things in return for their giving) is to be subtly rebellious toward the patient by refusing to be manipulated by their behavior (Cashdan 1988).

In dealing with the countertransference reactions that emerge as a result of the masochist's chronic caretaking, the therapist is advised to observe and process these patterns. For example, the therapist may say to the patient: "I appreciate how accommodating you are with me and how helpful you are to other group members but I am concerned that we are allowing you to be the caretaker with us the way you tend to be in your other relationships. My hunch is that this is not going to be helpful to you in the long run as it will keep you believing that we only like you because you are so giving and accommodating. Furthermore, it doesn't help you learn to get your needs met by us." It is our experience that statements of this nature are often met with sincere appreciation by these patients.

This chapter reviewed some common countertransference reactions experienced by therapists who treat masochistic patients. To the extent that therapists have masochistic characteristics themselves and/or have had a parent with masochistic issues, such countertransference issues are likely to be more extreme. It is hoped, however, that by alerting therapists to these issues they will be able to use their responses in ways that are productive for patients rather than unconsciously repeating the patients' previous injuries.

10

Case Review of a Preneurotic Masochistic Patient

In this chapter we present the case of a preneurotic masochistic patient and describe alternative therapeutic strategies that can be effective with particular masochistic presentations.

INITIAL PRESENTATION

Karen is a 35-year-old, single, white female who has two master's degrees and is a Ph.D. student in education. She works at a number of part-time jobs to pay her way through school. Karen is attractive, trim, very well groomed, and expensively dressed. She had not been in therapy previously and was referred to therapy by a friend who was worried about her after a recent breakup. She met with the therapist once a week for 15 months.

Karen presented herself initially in a friendly, dominant manner, looking confident and seeming like she "had it all together," although she was discussing painful problems. She opened the session by commenting on how the therapist must like to travel given the pictures on her wall.

The patient's manner was engaged, but self-contained. She anticipated when the session was coming to an end and asked the therapist if they needed to close for today about a minute before the session was over. Her second week in treatment she heard crying in the therapist's office before her session and subsequently began her own session by asking the therapist if she "would like to rest a little more before starting since the last session was probably hard."

PRESENTING PROBLEM

Karen reported that her most recent relationship had ended two weeks previously and that she was aware of repeating a relationship pattern that was very painful. She felt depressed and discouraged. She said that she tended to pick men who were unfaithful to her and then stayed in the relationship even after it became painful to her and was obviously deteriorating. She never left these relationships. In each case, after much lying, betrayal, and pain, the men left Karen for a new woman.

Karen realized that she tended to feel attracted to men who had similar characteristics: they all were in prestigious careers (such as medicine), earned a lot of money, and were self-absorbed or otherwise emotionally and physically unavailable and were often self-enhancing at Karen's expense. She felt good about herself in these relationships as long as she was in pursuit of winning them over and they were relatively aloof. She chose men on the basis of chemistry and "jumped into these relationships with both feet" before she really knew who her partners were. Even when she did know that they had a history of infidelity, she would get involved because she told herself "it won't happen to me."

Karen knew that she had trouble setting limits with people because she was afraid of making them angry. She also had a strong tendency to accommodate others. She frequently made friends by listening to their problems and doing things for them. For example, several of her friends tended to call her to talk about problems late at night and she would always listen patiently even when she had to get up early the next day. She put a lot of effort into being strong, appropriate, and competent.

Karen recognized that her self-esteem was low. She tended to dissect herself to try to find her flaws whenever she experienced conflict in her relationships. Her highly critical, probing self-examinations often caused her great anxiety that she somaticized into stomach ailments (e.g., indigestion, ulcers). She was reluctant, however, to seek medical attention when she had a problem as she feared that the doctors would think she was a "quack" and feel burdened by her.

HISTORY

Karen described her mother as "very temperamental," her father as "non-emotional," and herself as "a good girl" during her childhood. Her father had left her mother for another woman when Karen was 10 years old. Karen remembered feeling tremendous panic and abandonment as her favorite parent "dropped out of sight for years." Her mother told Karen that it was Karen's fault that her father left because "kids were such a burden." Karen had felt loved by her father, but that security was shaken by her mother's repeated admonitions: "How could you believe that? He left you, didn't he? Just like men, they're all babies. Just out for their own pleasure. You're stupid to believe them. I'm telling you this for your own good, Karen. Sometimes, if you really love your kids you have to tell them things that hurt them so that they'll know better next time."

Karen remembers hating her mother's verbal tirades and admiring her father's emotional containment. Karen decided to try to emulate her father despite her mother's protestations and admonitions. She chose an overachiever role in which to invest her self-esteem since she felt so insecure about her appearance and her person. She hoped to please her father through her achievements, but her emotional style downplayed her best efforts. When she told her father she was accepted into a Ph.D. program, he said,"Why do you have to do that when you have two master's degrees already?" In response, Karen initially felt deflated, but then became even more determined to prove herself to him.

The family atmosphere prior to the divorce appeared to be one of a verbal battleground. Post-divorce, the mother never remarried and appears to have settled into a state of strained bitterness. The father remarried and appears to have refocused his life except for periodic visits to see Karen while she was growing up.

Karen grew up "letting other people make me feel I'm wrong or too demanding. I've always doubted myself and so strove to be a better person so I would be attractive to someone good." Karen's first boyfriend was an alcoholic medical student whom she tried to rehabilitate for over two years. Her last boyfriend was a workaholic lawyer who treated her like she was a child because she was "still a student and not really out in the real world." Her relation- ships often lasted one to two years before they ended. She also kept in contact with her ex-boyfriends and made them into her friends so that she never really separated from them, physically or emotionally.

FORMULATION OF PROBLEM

Karen exhibited behaviors that indicated a masochistic character, structured at the preneurotic level of ego and object relations development. Her mother's proclivity to verbal abuse and devaluations in the guise of loving Karen, the general intolerance of separate opinions (e.g., Karen was pressured to hate and distrust her father just as her mother did), and the messages to "trust your mother not yourself" induced Karen to judge herself through other's eyes and to believe that love and suffering were naturally associated.

In areas of work and friendship, Karen appeared successful although at the expense of perfectionistic striv- ings and an entrenched caretaking style. However, in the romantic arena, where Karen overly relied on sexual at- traction in her decision making, she maintained a pattern of intractable, anxious attachments to men whom she admired for their social prestige, but who tended to exhibit narcissistic qualities (devaluation, self-absorption) that she thought represented strength of character (e.g., not needing anyone). She would take care of these men in the hopes that they would then take care of her. When this did not happen, she automatically assumed responsibility and searched for the defects in her person. At the prospect of a breakup, Karen would experience abandonment panic and

find herself unable to "get a perspective" or soothe herself.
When she called her friends for support, they often ended
up giving her the advice to stand up to the man, set limits,
or break up with him. "He wasn't good enough for you
anyway." She would then feel great empathy for the man
and take his point of view, abandoning herself in the
process. Ultimately, no matter what anyone said, Karen
believed the relationship problems were her fault and she
just needed to work harder. She focused on the times that
the men in her life were charming, tender, playful, or
vulnerable. Karen thus manifested a proclivity toward the
use of masochistic splitting in these relationships.

THERAPEUTIC GOALS AND THE COURSE OF THERAPY

Karen attended each of her sessions over the course of a
15-month period. She was always on time, usually arriving
5 to 10 minutes early. In the initial months of therapy,
Karen maintained a posture of nonobtrusive vigilance,
noticing empathically when the therapist looked stressed
(e.g., due to an emergency that had delayed her session 15
minutes) and apologizing profusely the rare times when
she had to change her appointment time given changes in
her school schedule.

Primary goals in working with Karen included offering a relationship that would help her attenuate her
depression, increase her capacity for object constancy
(self-soothing, self-regard) under stress and separation,
soften her harsh superego, support her strivings for individuation, and strengthen her observing ego when she felt
in conflict with others. The therapist attempted to function

in conflict with others. The therapist attempted to function as a nonreactive, interested, empathic auxiliary ego who would help Karen realistically normalize and regard herself when she lost the ability to do so. This approach was intended to facilitate the completion of Karen's internalizations of such adaptive ego functions as self-validation, compassion, comfort, empathy, and perspective so that she could more adequately self-soothe during separations and/or conflicts with significant others.

In the beginning months of therapy, the treatment focused on helping Karen (a) grieve over the loss of her last romantic relationship with a man named Patrick; (b) examine how she continued to resist setting limits with this man when he would contact her and try to reengage her, only to make promises he would not keep; (c) link her awareness of her romantic patterns to her family history; and (d) understand the power of her "romantic survival dream." At one point when Karen was feeling miserable over her longing for Patrick, the therapist observed that it seemed like a very old longing and that the therapist was never sure whether or not Karen really wanted Patrick, who disappointed her so often, or the dream of who she thought Patrick could be or used to be. Karen confirmed her own confusion and therapy was directed toward helping Karen differentiate the characteristics of her ideal object from the characteristics Patrick manifested.

Once the separation between Patrick and her ideal was completed, therapy was directed toward helping Karen see the cost of maintaining such a dream (while acknowledging how the ideal had provided hope of restitution and had thus helped her survive the loneliness and abuse of her family). As a result of making the ideal more conscious, Karen started the process of constructing more realistic and attainable aspirations for a romantic partnership. Mourning the loss of her childhood dream brought up many early painful memories from which the dream was supposed to save her.

In the middle of therapy, Karen met a man named Kevin, who was respectful, loving, and stable. Much of the rest of therapy focused on helping Karen to understand her reactions to Kevin and to help her differentiate transference feelings from how she felt about who he really was. Karen's relationship with her parents also came under examination as she began to see them and herself more realistically and grieve what she was never going to be able to get from them.

In terms of her new relationship with Kevin, Karen felt that she had finally found a man who really cared about her and she wrestled with feeling bored and devaluing of his stability and his willingness to take her into consideration. She divided men into two categories: strong, exciting, and self-absorbed or weak, boring, caring, and considerate. She found herself missing the excitement of longing, pursuing, and never knowing exactly where she stood with a man. The therapy focused on helping her to differentiate "strong" from "unemotional, and self-centered" and to redefine it as allowing oneself to be vulnerable, real, and expressive with loved ones.

Redefining what "strong" meant as well as loosening Karen's devaluations of "weak" helped her relax her defenses around her own feelings. As therapy progressed, she became more spontaneously expressive. With each expression, the therapist would track Karen's feelings of shame or embarrassment about her feelings. It became clear to both Karen and her therapist that her feelings about her feelings caused her more pain than did her original feelings. Feeling shame induced her to talk about her feelings as "weak and ugly." It took her months to understand at an emotional level the strength of vulnerability and the expression of feeling.

Karen had an ingrained tendency to overfocus on the negative and dismiss or minimize the positive. As a result the therapist actively watched for and pointed out her behavior and its effects. At one point, the therapist intervened: "I noticed that when you first started talking about the progress you've made in slowing down your relationships so you could really get to know each other before you gave your heart away, you smiled as if you were pleased with yourself. But when I asked you how you felt, you focused on your disappointment around how hard and frustrating this process is." Karen nodded affirmatively and the therapist continued: "Is it fair to say that this is a patterned way you have of reacting . . . that your attention goes to the most negative and discouraging aspects of your experience and neglects the more positive elements that exist?"

The other pattern that emerged in the middle of therapy manifested in Karen's tendency to dwell on how the therapeutic relationship was just not going to be able to help her because her "wild" or "bad" inclinations were too powerful. Karen particularly tended to focus on this feeling of "helplessness" whenever she was on the verge of or in the midst of some significant change (often related to deepening her commitment in the therapy or with Kevin). These manifestations eventually evoked countertransference feelings of temporary deadness, helplessness, tiredness, frustration, or irritation. Treating these feelings as possible reflections of Karen's projective identification processes helped both parties to better understand Karen's depressive stance and reorient her to a larger perspective. The therapist intervened in a number of ways, one of which was simply to note: "Your tendency to make the negative feelings you experience represent your whole experience leads me to wonder how demoralized you can feel over time." The therapist followed up this observation with questions that were aimed at linking present to past: "Is this a familiar feeling? When have you felt this way before?" Another intervention personalized the intended impact by noting: "I wonder if there is a part of you that has a hard time allowing yourself (and perhaps me) to be successful in here. If so, I wonder what the danger is in letting yourself be successful in relationships."

Once these patterns were acknowledged by Karen, the therapist focused on the advantages (e.g., preparing for the worst, illusion of control) as well as the costs (e.g., spoiling success, burning out on helping others) of this life stance. Once the ego-syntonicity of this stance had been rendered ego-dystonic, the therapist could help Karen focus on change by watching for and underscoring partial credit as well as empathizing with and accepting realistic shortcomings, mistakes, and failures. Helping Karen develop a realistic self-concept and a realistic, achievable ideal object represented substantial progress in her recovery from masochism.

The therapist also tracked Karen's ability to self-soothe and editorialize (or maintain observing ego) throughout the therapy. In the beginning months, when Karen seemed unable to maintain a realistic, larger perspective, the therapist would sometimes invite her to be a "fly on the wall" and comment on what she saw herself and other people experiencing (John Nardo, personal communication 1991). This technique was designed to help Karen distance herself from the intensity and selective focus of her experience so that she could enlarge her view.

Early in therapy, Karen also seemed unable to soothe herself around her reconnections and separations from her then ex-boyfriend, Patrick. In addition, she was unable to take full advantage of the therapist's help. For the most part, she tried to "gut it out" for fear of appearing "weak." During therapy sessions Karen would tend to minimize or ignore the therapist's empathic efforts. The therapist eventually pointed out how she tended to either change the subject or empathize with the person with whom she was experiencing conflict whenever the therapist offered Karen an observation that was meant to empathize with her. The therapist told Karen that it looked like it was difficult for her to take in the therapist's empathy and asked her, "If that's true, why might that be the case?"

Karen was able to talk about how her mother had exhibited a public style of false friendliness, complimenting people to their face, but criticizing them in private. Karen remembered one party where her mother complimented an old friend on how well she looked, only to talk about how old she looked after the party was over. Karen learned not to trust anything that felt positive. At other times she felt like the therapist was just trying "to motivate or manipulate" her. Karen had a hard time determining when people were really genuine and when they were not, but even when she thought the therapist was being sincere, she dismissed the offering by telling herself the therapist just did not know her well enough. Time was then spent in therapy slowing down the process by noting when Karen was dismissing potentially "good stuff," and inviting her to both check her "gut feeling" of genuineness and to let the feedback "sit for a bit before dismissing it to see what happens and determine what part, if any, fits and what part does not." Making the process more conscious helped Karen make more intentional rather than automatic, impulsive decisions. Intentionality helped to empower Karen, and slowing down the process helped her to internalize what felt valuable to her.

As Karen became more appreciative of the value of

empathy and validation she began the process of helping her friends understand what she needed (e.g., empathy rather than advice) and talking to herself in the way she experienced the therapist talking to her. At one point in the last months of therapy, she noted that one night she felt panicky over the prospect of marrying her boyfriend. She worried that she could be making a terrible mistake, giving up the prospect of excitement and thrills for the rest of her life. She then realized that her therapist would probably tell her that these might be old feelings and were expectable every once in a while given her history. Those feelings did not have to mean she should break up with him. She reminded herself that she tended to catastrophize at these times and that if she does not scare herself and if she listens to herself she will come to know what's in her best interest over time. Karen noted that "this self-talk calmed me down."

Therapy ended arbitrarily with Karen's graduation and her subsequent move to a new location due to new employment. She was still early in the process of completing self-regulating transmuting internalizations. Self-soothing internalizations, for example, were not yet metabolized into her own self-functions but remained as identifications with her therapist. Termination was difficult for Karen. She tended to avoid direct discussions of her experience with the therapist and how she was feeling about the impending loss. When the therapist noted that she seemed to be bringing in mini-crises that took all their attention so they did not have much time to say good-bye to each other, Karen became uncomfortable, smiled, and said "I know" in a low voice. She then became very sad and let herself cry appropriately, noting how full of feeling, appreciation, loss, and even anger she was. Karen was able to let the therapist know that she was angry that the therapy was ending prematurely although she realized it was no one's fault, but rather a side result of her success. She realized this pain of separation and loss is what she had been trying to avoid. She could talk about what aspects of her therapy experience she was going to be able to take with her (e.g., "I talk to you in my head now") and what she would grieve. Together Karen and the therapist reminisced, underscoring her progress over the past 15 months, with an eye focused on articulating what Karen's current growing edges were so that once she was settled in her new location she would be able to continue therapy with more clarity regarding her goals for further treatment. Karen knew that she still needed help to sort out the meaning of her feelings as she worked through her continuing issues with intimacy and separation. However, she now had a "good enough" base of trust in herself and the therapeutic process that she felt substantially assured that she would continue to work through her issues, particularly the intense fears that still periodically swept over her as she both allowed herself to receive assistance and love from Kevin and to develop further confidence in herself.

11

Differential Diagnosis

The accurate, evolving diagnosis of a patient is critical to establishing effective treatment goals and strategies. This therapeutic task is complicated, however, by the fact that models like the *DSM-IV* employ a symptom-based, descriptive approach that does not address ego-structural issues or psychodynamic theory. In addition many patients exhibit symptomatology in more than one diagnostic category (Benjamin 1993), which can make differential diagnosis even more difficult.

Unlike the atheoretical *DSM-IV*, the psychodynamic/object relations-based model presented in this book does facilitate the establishment of a treatment plan. Psychodynamic models, however, are generally less quantifiable than the behaviorally based *DSM-IV*, making differential diagnosis even more difficult. For example, whether a phenomenon is labeled splitting or ambivalence often entails a measure of subjective interpretation.

Clear object relations-based guidelines for differentiating structure and character organization are thus crucial to accurate diagnosis and effective treatment planning. In Chapter 4 we specifically outlined how to differentiate the masochistic character structured at the preneurotic level of ego/object relations development from this character disorder structured at the borderline and neurotic levels. In this chapter, we describe specific guidelines regarding how to distinguish the preneurotic masochistic character from five other character disorders that share common symptomatology with the masochistic character: narcissistic, paranoid, obsessive-compulsive, hysteric, and hysteroid personalities.

SIMILARITIES AMONG SHAME-BASED CHARACTER STYLES

The preneurotic masochistic, narcissistic, paranoid, and obsessive-compulsive personalities share important elements of their core identity organization that propel a number of similar symptoms. This shared pool of similar symptomatology is part of what makes differential diagnosis particularly confusing. After a brief overview of these four personalities, the narcissistic, paranoid, and obsessive-compulsive character styles will be individually contrasted to the masochistic personality. When these analyses are completed the masochistic personality will then be compared to the hysteric and hysteroid character styles.

Confusing the narcissistic, paranoid, and obsessive-compulsive personalities with the masochistic character occurs in part because all four of these personalities are structured around a shame-based core identity or real self.

The hysteric individual, in contrast, manifests a guilt-based personality while the hysteroid largely manifests a deficit-based personality whereby identity-diffusion and feelings of emptiness form the core sense of self. Shame is relevant for the hysteroid insomuch as this character structure has sufficiently developed a core self organization that can invest in being valued by another whose opinions related to the self are highly regarded.

By and large, shame-based personalities devalue who they are, while guilt-based personalities unconsciously believe they should be punished for what they have done. In addition, shame-based personalities generally feel compelled to conceal their underlying sensitivity and pain, and are often quite able to do so while their defenses are intact.

Furthermore, these four shame-based personalities feel propelled by perfectionistic strivings in an unconscious effort to avoid or control the intense discomfort associated with how they really feel about themselves. Masochistic and obsessive-compulsive personalities tend to employ perfectionism in the service of internal security operations, while the narcissistic and paranoid personalities employ perfectionism more in the service of self-esteem.

In terms of further differential criteria, each of these personalities manifests a somewhat different form of perfectionism. For example, obsessive-compulsives are often compelled to do things perfectly correct in order to feel the security of being right (Salzman 1980, Wells et al. 1990). In contrast, masochists strive to be perfectly good and giving in order to earn the love and approval of a security object (Glickauf-Hughes and Wells 1991). Paranoids strive to be perfectly above reproach in order to secure self-approval in a dangerous and unjustly critical world (Meissner 1978). Finally, narcissists desire to be naturally perfect in their beauty or talents or brilliance in order to bask in the admiration of their audiences (Glickauf-Hughes and Wells 1991).

These personalities thus typically induce through their perfectionism some amount of irritation in others. For example, with obsessives, others (including the therapist) can sometimes wish these individuals would loosen up or give themselves and others a break. With masochists others can feel like saying, "Why do you put up with that over and over again" or "You can do so much better than so-and-so." With paranoids others can find themselves thinking, "Take some responsibility for yourself. It's not always somebody else's fault." With narcissists others can feel like saying, "See me. There are two people in this relationship, you know." While these statements are presented in a tongue-in-cheek or caricatured manner, they capture an essence of one of the most useful differential diagnosis criteria—the therapist's reaction to the patient's presentation.

The interpersonal impact of each of these personalities infers important motivational and structural elements of their intrapsychic operations. For example, the obsessive's press for perfectly correct behavior in others and the self reflects an excessively harsh superego. The masochist's repeated return to security relationships that hurt him or her infers an intrapsychic structure of incomplete transmuting internalizations and a proclivity to internalize blame. The paranoid's litigious, blaming behavior infers an overdetermined focus on the preservation of the self and a proclivity to externalize blame. The narcissist operates out of a grandiose false self stance that negates the separateness of the other person in order to use the other as a needed selfobject (e.g., "You and I want what I want because I want it and I need you to want it in order to validate my self-initiations").

All four of these personalities can, in fact, present with grandiosity, although, as with perfectionism, the manifestation or form that the grandiosity takes will differ from one personality style to another in a predictable fashion. The grandiosity of each personality reflects the area of perfectionistic strivings upon which they overfocus their efforts. In caricature form, masochists can express their grandiosity around the illusion of being "Gandhi-like" (i.e., someone who essentially starves him/herself in the service of others). In contrast, obsessives can express their grandiosity around "Mr. Spock–like" presentations of ultra-reasonableness, controlled affect, and correctness. Paranoids can manifest grandiosity in a "Stalin-like" manner (i.e., someone who constantly purged himself of his own ranks of loyal officers because of his intense unfounded suspicions). Narcissists can manifest their grandiosity around "Mohammed Ali–like" illusions of being "the greatest."

Having compared and contrasted the common core identity elements of the four shame-based personalities and their shared symptomatology, we turn directed to a series of individual analyses comparing the masochistic personality with the narcissistic, paranoid, and obsessive-compulsive personalities. In the final section of the chapter we compare and contrast the preneurotic masochistic character to the more mature neurotic-level hysterical personality and the more immature borderline hysteroid personality.

THE MASOCHISTIC AND THE NARCISSISTIC PERSONALITY

These two character styles are often particularly difficult to differentiate for a number of reasons: (a) preneurotic and borderline structured masochism include narcissistic self components, (b) masochistic and narcissistic character styles represent counterparts or mirror images of each other (Seiden 1989), and (c) these two character styles are often structured at the same preneurotic level of ego/object relations development and thus share common structural weaknesses that dominate the early phases of therapy. Horner (1979) has noted that narcissistic and masochistic personalities have similar structural organizations. What is particularly confusing is that masochistic relationship patterns can and often do serve narcissistic self needs (Stolorow 1975), especially at the preneurotic and border-line levels of ego/object relations development where struc-tural issues take motivational precedence over dynamic conflicts. Masochistic relationship patterns also reflect substantial and early narcissistic wounds, which leave the individual searching for the means to assure self-security, cohesion, and self-esteem. As a result the preneurotic masochist often chooses significant others on the basis of narcissistic criteria (e.g., how the person physically looks, what the other provides, how the other makes them feel) and relies on the relationship to provide ego functions for which the masochist cannot rely on the self due to incom-plete transmuting internalizations of internal security and self-esteem.

The question thus arises as to how the clinician can differentiate the masochistic character style used to gratify certain underlying narcissistic self needs from the pure narcissistic character (Cooper 1988). This question is com-plicated by the fact that masochistic and narcissistic indi-viduals also share a number of personality characteristics, including perfectionistic strivings, the need to feel special, feelings of grandiosity or insignificance, and hypersensi-tivity to the evaluation of others.

One way to differentiate the masochistic from the narcissistic individual is to remember that although they share the aformentioned personality issues these issues are typically exhibited in complementary fashion in the masochist and narcissist. For example, both character types are excessively sensitive to criticism, but the narcissist usually rejects or devalues critics while the masochist typically tries even harder to please critics in order to win them over.

The authors believe that the prototype for understanding the difference between masochists and narcissists is succinctly expressed in Greco-Roman mythology through the story of Narcissus and Echo. In this myth, both Echo and Narcissus overfocus on Narcissus' image. In the process Echo disowns her own healthy narcissism while Narcissus disowns his ability to empathize with others. As a result each has part of what the other desperately needs but does not focus on developing within the self.

We now examine in detail how each of the character issues that these two personalities share in common are expressed differently. With regard to perfectionistic strivings, masochists tend to strive for a feeling of worthiness or being deserving through being good and giving, while narcissists strive to be perfect because they are, quite simply, the greatest (e.g., the most beautiful, admirable, talented). The unconscious motivations that underlie these strivings are also different for the masochist and the narcissist. The masochist wants to earn love through being above reproach and perfectly deserving. The narcissist, on the other hand, wants to be perfect so as to bask in the world's admiration. When the world offers each of these personalities the love and admiration they so desperately seek, they each respond quite differently. The masochist typically feels a sense of deep appreciation, while the narcissist responds as if such admiration were simply his or her due (Kernberg 1975).

In addition, the authors have noted that in terms of underlying priorities, masochists and narcissists are organized differently. Narcissists will thus give up relationships in order to preserve their fragile sense of self-esteem, while masochists will give up self-esteem in order to maintain a security relationship (Glickauf-Hughes and Wells 1991). Narcissists thus tend to externalize responsibility for any wrongdoing and only rarely apologize. Masochists, on the other hand, tend to immediately internalize wrongdoing or fault and automatically apologize. One of the hallmarks of the masochistic character is, in fact, the symptom of apologizing without even really knowing what one is apologizing for.

Despite these differences it should be remembered that both the masochist and the narcissist have given up on attending to or developing their real selves and so never feel a sense of lasting self-worth. Typically, however, the preneurotic masochist has a somewhat more developed sense of real self than the narcissist, who overrelies on an inflated or grandiose false self in order to sustain esteem or narcissistic equilibrium. We agree with Johnson's (1985) theory that this is due in part to the masochist's will being derailed at a later stage of separation-individuation than that of the narcissist.

In addition, narcissists tend to use others for selfobject functions to a greater extent than do masochists. We hypothesize that this theory may account for the masochist's greater capacity for genuine object love and emotional empathy. Narcissists, while capable of intellectual empathy, have great difficulty with emotional empathy whenever their own needs are not being met. This limitation constricts the narcissist's capacity for real object love. This lack of emotional empathy is often reflected in the narcissist's apparent search for fatal flaws in intimate relationships. These fatal flaws allow the narcissist to devalue the significant other and distance him or herself in the relationship in the face of any possible narcissistic injury. This defensive style seems to provide an inducement for the masochist to become determined to win back the rejecting narcissist in order to regain "paradise lost."

MASOCHISTIC AND PARANOID CHARACTER STYLES

Like the narcissistic character, the paranoid character (Nydes 1963) has been formulated as a polarity with the masochistic character. Nydes proposes that "the masochistic character appears to renounce 'power' for the sake of 'love'; and the paranoid character appears to renounce 'love' for the sake of 'power'" (p. 56). Differential diagnosis is difficult because these two disorders share a number of symptoms: (a) being unaware of provoking what one fears; (b) identifying with the victim role; (c) displaying compensatory feelings of grandiosity that defend against (d) underlying feelings of inadequacy, inferiority (Sullivan 1953), and depression; (e) expecting punishment for any form of self-assertion or real success (Meissner 1989), and (f) displaying impaired autonomy (Aronson 1989, Glick and Meyers 1988). The fact that these two character formulations can combine in a mixed personality disorder (Meissner 1989, Nydes 1963) can also confuse diagnostic matters. Finally, masochistic and paranoid personalities are sometimes attracted to each other due to the complementarity of their dynamics and worldview.

Whether played out on an intrapsychic level or on an

interpersonal level, the dynamics between the masochistic and paranoid personality styles often fit hand-in-glove. The masochist retains a proclivity to internalize responsibility and blame in order to maintain an illusion of control over the self's perceived badness and to protect the goodness of the security object. This proclivity complements the paranoid's proclivity to externalize and project responsibility and blame onto the other, thus turning the self into the victim of persecution or mistreatment and in this manner protecting a feeling of internal goodness. In this dynamic the masochist identifies the self with a sadistic agent who should be punished while the paranoid identifies the self as a persecuted victim who should be avenged. Meissner (1989) notes that often in this interpersonal pairing it is the masochistic spouse who finally seeks therapy due to the unbearable demands at home while the paranoid partner resists any suggestion of treatment.

The masochist and the paranoid personalities are not fully conscious of how they provoke what they fear in others. For example, masochists do not understand how their excessive helpfulness or overinvolvement might be experienced as intrusive, especially by those individuals who are sensitive to control and power issues. Paranoid personalities, on the other hand, are not aware of how their demandingness, controlling tendencies, and rigidity can induce irritations. Both masochists and paranoid personalities induce the world to treat them in such a way as to confirm their worldview. For the masochist, this view has to do with being bad or not good enough no matter how hard they try in a good or otherwise gratifying world. For the paranoid this view has to do with being the persecuted innocent or the unjustly accused in a dangerous world.

If we scratch the surface of masochists we can see the centrality of their victim identifications. On the other hand, if we scratch the surface of paranoids we can also see their intense feelings of worthlessness, personal inadequacy, and inferiority. These mirror dynamics are part of what can make the differential diagnosis of these two personalities very difficult at times.

Paranoid and masochistic personalities are thus closely related in a number of ways. Fenichel (1945) wrote of how paranoid delusions served to relieve the individual from feelings of shame, guilt, inadequacy, or the masochistic stance of turning aggression against the self through the mechanism of projection. Bak (1946) related paranoia to a state of delusional masochism. In this conceptualization the withdrawal of libido and increased aggression toward the love object accompanies regression to masochism or identification with unjustified victim status. However, Nydes (1963) differentiated masochism and paranoia by the priority of power and love in their motivational system (see above).

MASOCHISTIC AND OBSESSIVE-COMPULSIVE PERSONALITIES

Masochistic and obsessive-compulsive personalities struggle with related vulnerabilities around autonomy and individuation. As a result of mutual proclivities, the masochistic and obsessive individuals are prone to power struggles with each other. Masochists tend to misinterpret the obsessives' desire to have everyone do things the "correct" way as manifesting narcissistic selfishness. The obsessive tends to misinterpret the masochist's desire to win the obsessive over, in order to feel safe and secure, as being picky, demanding, and condescending criticism. Both see the other through transference filters that tend to distort who the other really is.

Masochists tend to be more interpersonally oriented, whereas obsessives are generally more superego oriented (Glickauf-Hughes and Wells 1991). As a result, masochists tend to give up self-esteem in order to maintain their security relationship while obsessives tend to give up getting along with others in order to retain the approval of their superego demands. The masochistic personality's defensive tactic is intended to reduce separation anxiety and feelings of loss (Avery 1977). In contrast, the obsessive personality's defensive style is aimed at reducing castration anxiety (Salzman 1980). Both styles are intended to ensure the illusion of external security and internal control over what cannot be controlled in life.

The differences between the masochistic and obsessive-compulsive style stem in part from the differences in the parenting styles that they encountered in their families of origin. Masochists tend to have one parent who is highly controlling in an irrational, unpredictable manner that is largely lacking in self-discipline, and another parent who adapts to this presentation by trying to smooth the rough waters. The one parent is often seen as exciting but hurtful while the other is seen as a self-sacrificing saint who manipulates through guilt. Obsessive-compulsives tend to have at least one self-contained, reserved, rule-bound parent who is controlling in a more predictable, rigid, and authoritarian manner. Obsessives tend to have more stable family backgrounds than masochists and thus tend to have been able to achieve greater libidinal object constancy.

THE MASOCHISTIC AND HYSTERIC/ HYSTEROID PERSONALITIES

The preneurotic masochistic personality can have features in common with both ends of the hysteric continuum: the more mature, essentially neurotic hysterical personality and the more immature, borderline hysteroid personality. The clinician thus needs to be able to differentiate the masochistic personality from both the hysterical and the hysteroid characters. Like hysterical personality development, masochistic personality development has been described on a continuum, ranging from nonpathological to various degrees of pathology from neurotic to borderline. The nonpathological personality-style descriptions indicate the socially oriented strengths of each personality. The nonpathological hysterical style includes a global or holistic cognitive style, a relational orientation, and an affective responsiveness. The nonpathological masochistic style, on the other hand, includes a relational orientation, a willingness to persevere or endure in order to achieve the greater good, and a principled orientation. The essence of these descriptions reflect the diversity of socially promoted proclivities and the potential opportunities for complementarity in relationships.

In terms of the more mature pathological substitutes (specifically at the preneurotic and/or neurotic levels), we again find both the masochistic and the hysterical personality are highly relational, but the tendency toward an other orientation is manifested in an excessive need to please others in order to gain love and approval. Both masochistic and hysterical personality types tend to be romantic, idealizing their love objects and blaming themselves for relationship problems. The masochist and the hysteric were raised in family systems that led them to believe that their principal value in life was to cater to self-absorbed parents (e.g., Glickauf-Hughes and Wells 1991, Mueller and Aniskiewicz 1986). As a result, both personalities tend to function as the family negotiator and/or nurturer and were trained to sacrifice their independence and strivings for individuation for the sake of a relationship. The masochist, however, typically offers these functions in the role of a serious, overresponsible caretaker, while the hysteric tends to offer these functions in the role of a charming provocative and/or seductive child.

Both personalities choose roles that are designed to help them to feel secure in relationships with an important other. Both fear dependency and vulnerability because it has become associated with being controlled. The masochist tends to try to avoid dependency and vulnerability in relationships by assuming a counterdependent style and adhering to the dominant role of caretaker. The hysteric, on the other hand, tries to avoid being genuinely dependent by "acting" helpless and "demanding" care, and avoids vulnerability by "feigning" fragility (Mueller and Aniskiewicz 1986, p. 59). Masochists believe they can only be loved by earning it through being indispensable or needed. Hysterics, on the other hand, believe that the way to be loved is through dramatic or seductive charm and passive-dependency.

Both the hysteric and the masochist fight feeling too much because intense feelings are experienced as indicating a weakness in character. For the hysteric, this fight is witnessed as a particular paradox as the hysteric uses pseudoemotional expressiveness as a cover for real feelings while the masochist uses overcontainment as a defense against the feelings of vulnerability that arise with emotional self-expression.

Both the hysteric and the masochist have been described as wrestling with (a) compliance and willfulness; (b) issues of control and manipulation; (c) themes of victimization, helplessness, and irresponsibility; and (d) mistrust (Mueller and Aniskiewicz 1986). In both cases their compliance and willfulness can be attributed to their ability to fight off more severe pathology (Mueller and

Aniskiewicz 1986). The hysterical personality often reflects a willful noncompliance with authority figures (e.g.,
parents or teachers). The hysteric's compliance is usually
observed with his or her chosen peer group and represents
his or her strivings toward individuation. While the hysterical patient may be waging autonomy wars in the wrong
arena with undesirable outcomes, "until the underlining
matters are rectified in psychotherapy, the fight itself is
emotionally healthier than the dynamic implications of
submitting" (Mueller and Aniskiewicz 1986, p. 88).

The masochist's compliance is directed differently
than the hysteric's. The masochist overtly complies in
primary adult relationships in order to earn love rather
than rebelling with a peer group against family values in
order to strive for a sense of individuality. The masochist
strives for individuality through passive aggressive or
passive resistive behaviors with the same primary objects
with which he or she complies as opposed to rebelling with
one object against another.

Hysterics seek mutuality in relationship and use compliance as a bargaining chip in the striving for reciprocity.
They will go along with the other in the hopes of negotiating something reciprocal. This strategy is admittedly
something less than ideal mutuality, but the hysterical
personality has not had much practice with mature relationships (Mueller and Aniskiewicz 1986). If the therapist
interprets these attempts to gain equality as manipulation,
the hysteric's underlying issue is missed. If the hysterical
patient's demands are understood as a resistance to being
the one who must always submit, then the therapist may
approach the client with a "more respectful attitude and
'mutually' work . . . on how to achieve a more mature
mutuality" (Mueller and Aniskiewicz 1986, p. 90). In contrast, the masochist primarily seeks a sense of security in
relationships and complies with the other in hopes of

negotiating security at the expense of genuine self-expression.

Another potentially confusing area in differentiating the masochist and hysterical patient is that both may present with triangular relationships. For hysterics, however, the triad is often manifested through competition or jealousy with a third party while with masochists the triadic relationship is evidenced in the phenomenon of masochistic triangulation (i.e. victim, persecutor, rescuer) as discussed in Chapter 4. The therapist thus needs to be alert to these distinctions in order to correctly interpret the patient's motivations behind triangulating behavior.

In contrast to the neurotic hysteric, the hysteroid or borderline personality is more impulsive and emotionally labile. The hysteroid also features more sadomasochistic characteristics, and thus manifests more aggressive tendencies as outlined in Chapter 4. These distinctions can be particularly confusing for the beginning therapist who may misunderstand a hysteroid's initial presentation of apparent masochistic behaviors as indicating a basic masochistic character structure. In these cases, the therapist needs to pay special attention to the underlying structural deficits as well as to the motivational context for the behavioral display.

For example, both the preneurotic masochist and the borderline hysteroid personality have unresolved separation-individuation issues that manifest in incomplete libidinal object constancy. This developmental deficit results in chronic overdependence on others to serve as auxiliary egos to provide the internal security operations these character disorders cannot provide for themselves. The developmental arrest, however, is significantly earlier in hysteroids than in masochists. While masochists' development has been arrested at the final stage of separation-individuation, the "child on the way to object constancy" (Johnson 1985), the hysteroids' development has been arrested in the symbiotic, hatching, and rapprochement stages of separation-individuation (Horner 1979). As a result masochists struggle with incomplete transmuting internalizations and insufficient object constancy and self-soothing abilities. In contrast, hysteroids suffer from more severe self-integrative and self-cohesive deficits (Kernberg 1975) that are manifested in identity diffusion, impulse control problems, and the potentiality for brief psychotic episodes under sufficient stress.

Masochists can thus tolerate minor separations and primarily manifest separation anxiety in relation to the possible ending of a relationship with an idealized significant other. Hysteroids, on the other hand, experience more global difficulty with a range of both real and perceived separations and frustrations. A hysteroid can, for example, become very distressed, even suicidal, over a perceived empathic failure or the therapist's pending absence during a planned vacation (Chessick 1983). Preneurotic masochists would generally respond quite differently, often by excessively apologizing for their very realistic needs and desires. For example, one masochist apologized to the therapist for needing a third Kleenex during a very cathartic session in which she was appropriately crying over her father's death. The patient reported that she felt bad about having to use up all the therapist's Kleenex.

In a related manner, while both masochists and hysteroids can manifest intense affects and depression, masochists usually can modulate their affects more effectively than borderline hysteroids are able to do. In addition, masochists generally use primitive defenses such as splitting and projective identification on a much more delimited basis than hysteroids. As discussed in Chapter 4, preneurotic masochists use splitting in a very particular manner with significant others, while hysteroids use global splitting across situations and relationships.

A final distinction between masochists and hysteroids is exhibited in social and occupational functioning (Glickauf-Hughes and Wells 1991). Hysteroids typically exhibit erratic, volatile, or intense short-term relationships that end in disillusionment and are discarded as a new need-gratifying object is designated. Hysteroids generally do not wait for relationships to develop naturally due to their pressing interpersonal need for an auxiliary ego. Furthermore, their closer relationships are generally not maintained long term because of their excessive neediness, underdeveloped frustration tolerance, and their use of splitting as a defense against any uncomfortable affect. Hysteroids thus seek saviors only to become understandably frustrated when they are let down. They then tend to vilify these designated saviors and discard them for another designated savior. Hyteroids may also develop occupational histories that reflect the same dynamics and deficits.

When preneurotic masochists manifest relational problems, they do so in a manner quite different than do hysteroids. For example, while hysteroids have problems committing to long-term relationship, masochists are generally quite capable of developing and maintaining in-depth long-term relationships. Masochists, however, find it difficult to leave a significant other who has been invested in as a security object, even when she or he is rejecting and abusive. Masochists thus tend to tolerate excessive frustration due to their difficulty setting appropriate limits, their deficient internal security operations, their counterdependent proclivities, and their rigid defense system (Glickauf-Hughes and Wells 1991). By contrast, hysteroids tend to have insufficient boundaries and defenses for dealing with the anxieties and challenges of life.

This chapter introduced several analyses comparing the preneurotic masochistic character to five other character organizations that share common symptomatology with the masochist. All clinicians need to familiarize themselves with explicit differentiating criteria to ensure more accurate diagnosis and related treatment strategies.

12

Dynamics and Treatment of the Masochistic-Narcissistic Couple

Historically, clinicians have noticed typical patterns of personality traits co-occurring in couples (Martin and Bird 1959) including patterns of complementary character structures and personality types (Klimek 1979). Noteworthy has been the observation that obsessive-compulsive personalities tend to form partnerships with hysterical personalities (Barnett 1971). However, as cultures change so do the prevailing character structures that emerge (Lasch 1978). This includes the type of pairings that clinicians observe among couples. One current pattern mentioned in the literature is that of the borderline-narcissistic couple (Lachkar 1985). We have also noted a propensity for individuals with a masochistic or self-defeating personality disorder to form alliances with individuals that have a narcissistic personality organization. While this pattern has been commonly observed in the popular psychology literature (Forward 1986, Norwood

1985), it has not to date been addressed in the professional literature.

SELF PSYCHOLOGY AND MARITAL RELATIONS

The ideas of self psychology, particularly Heinz Kohut's (1971) notion of selfobjects and self disorders, provide insight into the ways in which early childhood experiences have impact on adult marital relations. It has been frequently observed in discussions of contemporary marital problems that one or both partners suffer from disorders of the self (Schwartzman 1984, Solomon 1985, 1988). Individuals with self disorders have insufficient differentiation between self and others and tend to use one another as selfobjects. "The term 'selfobject' as applied to marital relationships refers to the use of another as a vehicle for maintaining, restoring or consolidating the internal experience of the self" (Solomon 1988, p. 213). Common selfobject functions include empathy, mirroring, admiration, and soothing.

In normal development, all children need affirmation of their accomplishments for the development of a sense of identity and self-esteem. Kohut (1971, 1977) believes that disorders of the self (e.g., enfeebled or fragmented selves, inadequate self-esteem regulation) result from the maternal figure's inability to provide good-enough selfobject functions during the child's early development. Couples in which one or both members have self disorders often have difficulty with normal problem solving, communication, and negotiations. "When there is a prior history of narcissistic vulnerability and failure of the other to provide necessary emotional supplies, the result is that small arguments may cause an experience of fragmentation, or emotional destruction, a loss of ability to think clearly and a reaction of either rage or total withdrawal" (Solomon 1988, p. 212). Furthermore, the failure of one partner to function as an admiring or idealized object to the other may cause narcissistic injury leading to depression as well as rage (Schwartzman 1984).

OBJECT RELATIONS THEORY AND MARITAL THERAPY

In recent years, there has been the beginning of a rapprochement between family therapy and object relations theory (Slipp 1984). In particular, both fields of study "are concerned with internal and external boundaries and the transfer of supplies across those boundaries" (Hamilton 1988, p. 308). The ideas of Klein (1975), Winnicott (1965), and Mahler and colleagues (1975) have begun to be integrated into conjoint family therapy. McCormack (1984) discusses the importance of the therapist serving as a "holding environment" (Winnicott 1965) in treating borderline-schizoid couples. In such a role, the therapist provides a sense of safety for the couple by giving ego support to both members and by being a neutral figure who contributes to the interactions with more rational, secondary-process thinking (McCormack 1984). Slipp (1984) discusses the importance of the concept, "projective identification" (Klein 1975) in understanding family dynamics. Projective identification is defined by Grotstein (1981) as "a mental mechanism whereby the self experiences the unconscious fantasies of translocating itself or aspects of itself, into an object for exploratory or defensive purposes" (p. 173). The individual thus attempts to master painful feelings by getting rid of them and placing them in a "bad" outside object. In addition, in projective identification, the individual frequently behaves in such a manner as to actually induce the unwanted aspect of the self into the object (e.g., making the object angry). McCormack believes that the therapist's ability to contain projective identifications is an important aspect of managing the holding environment. In this function, therapists recognize and understand the meaning of the countertransference feelings that they experience as a result of the patient's projective identifications, but do not act them out.

From a self psychology and object relations perspective, this chapter briefly reviews the salient characteristics of the masochistic (or self-defeating) personality and narcissistic personality disorders, attempts to describe and explain the characteristic relationship patterns that masochistic-narcissistic couples form throughout different stages of the relationship, and briefly addresses some important aspects of psychotherapy that are of particular concern in the treatment of these couples. The clinical observations that are described are based upon the treatment of approximately twenty couples in which one member has predominantly masochistic and the other member predominantly narcissistic dynamics.

THE MASOCHISTIC PERSONALITY

The masochistic personality is self-depreciating, self-sacrificing, and overtly pleasing but inwardly willful and angry (Johnson 1985). Masochists wish for the submission of their will to an idealized other (Menaker 1953). However, while they wish for love and idealized symbiosis (Smirnoff 1969), they fear that if they submit to another they will be humiliated or abandoned. The masochist thus has great difficulty receiving from others.

Although masochists have a relatively differentiated sense of self, they have great difficulty with self-esteem regulation. When in conflict with a significant other, they tend to essentially blame themselves and believe that if their partner is angry at them, they must be bad.

One of the primary conflict areas for the masochist is loss and separation (Avery 1977). Leaving their significant other seems so frightening to masochists that they prefer to distort their perceptions of their partner through denial and rationalization rather than leave him or her. Masochists believe that the pain they experience in their troubled relationships is far less than the overwhelming pain that they anticipate feeling if they left their partner.

MASOCHISTIC RELATIONAL GOALS AND FANTASIES

The masochist tends to be a romantic who survived a frequently abusive childhood through the use of fantasy in general and through dreams of ideal love in particular. In romantic relationships, masochists tend to assume a "regressive narcissistic role" (Willi 1982). In essence, they project their ideal self onto their partner and then identify with it, substituting it for their own devalued self. For example, one masochistic patient was mildly obese as a child in a family that placed great value upon physical appearance. During courtship with his wife, he was delighted that a slender, attractive woman was romantically interested in him. He reported feeling more attractive as though her beauty radiated onto him. In general, masochists have a tendency to choose partners who have virtues that they believe to be both highly desirable and most deficient in themselves.

The second characteristic that masochists are drawn to in partners is sensitivity to and empathic attunement with their unstated needs. Masochists wish for a love object who understands their deepest feelings and wishes without their even having to express them. For example, one masochistic partner was quite taken by a colleague who would come to her office at the end of the day and ask her if she would like to talk about her day. The desire to have one's unexpressed needs known and gratified, in part, meets the masochist's wish to attain fusion with the primary object with whom he or she feels an impossible separation (Smirnoff 1969).

Furthermore, due to masochists' rigid boundaries (as well as their wish for idealized symbiosis), they tend to be drawn to partners who express and elicit intense affect and who have a propensity to merge in relationships. Furthermore, as pain is more likely to permeate the masochist's rigid boundaries, the masochist is most often drawn to intense, dramatic, seemingly larger-than-life characters who sweep them up in a whirlwind courtship and then hurt them. Strong sexual attraction is an important component of this pattern.

Finally, a deep-seated wish for the masochist is to heal an old narcissistic injury by making the critical and/or rejecting parent (or parent substitute) love and approve of them (Berliner 1947). As such, masochists tend to be drawn to individuals who either seem unavailable or difficult to obtain. One masochistic patient talked about only being attracted to women that were a challenge for him. Furthermore, this patient (and masochistic patients in general) tended to devalue partners who wanted him. This pattern occurs because (a) masochists tend to confuse the experiences of love and longing, and (b) the masochist's aim is not a reunion with the loving mother but a fanta-sized control over a cruel and damaging mother (Cooper and Fischer 1981).

THE MASOCHIST DURING COURTSHIP

In the beginning of the relationship, in return for the love of the partner who they admire, masochists are willing to act as their partner's caretaker. In general, masochists tend to treat others as they wish to be treated themselves. They assume the caretaking role in relationships as (a) they believe that they are only loved for what they do for others rather than for who they are, and (b) they are more comfortable in the dominant, caretaking role in which they experience greater control in the process of giving and taking. Caretaking thus becomes a means of getting their own needs met vicariously without being vulnerable. The masochist thus begins to assume the role in their partner's life of attending to unwanted business and responsibilities. For example, one masochistic patient who was dating a professor devoted herself to him (e.g., cooking, cleaning, running his errands, editing his manuscripts) so that he was free to fulfill his intellectual potential. These responsi-bilities were assumed in spite of the fact that she held a professional position herself.

The second function that the masochist assumes in the beginning of relationships is that of a selfobject. In this capacity, masochists act as an extension of their partners providing them with psychological functions externally that they are unable to perform to a sufficient degree internally. For example, masochists initially idealize and admire their partners, colluding with their grandiose fan-tasies and shoring up their fragile self-esteem. Furthermore, they frequently assume the role of empathic listener, helping to soothe their partners when they are having difficulties and are unable to soothe themselves. Finally, they provide their partners with the mirroring and echoing that they so desperately need in order to support their precarious sense of self.

In sum, during courtship masochists are drawn to romantic, intense love objects who have qualities that they idealize but find deficient in themselves. It is important to masochists that their partners are empathically attuned with and responsive to their unspoken needs. In return for the love of their idealized objects, they are willing to function as their partner's caretaker and selfobject, providing him or her with help in daily living, comfort, and above all with admiration.

THE NARCISSISTIC PERSONALITY

Descriptive Clinical Overview

The narcissistic personality disorder as defined in the *DSM-IV* (APA 1994) includes the following relevant features: (a) need for constant attention, (b) feelings of entitlement, (c) interpersonal exploitiveness, (d) an ambition that cannot be satisfied, (e) preoccupation with grooming and remaining youthful, and (f) grandiosity. The narcissistic personality also feels omnipotent as well as grandiose (Masterson 1981). Narcissists try to be perfect (Glickauf-Hughes et al. 1987) and tend to be more concerned about other's opinions of them than about their own emotions. They have strong feelings of inferiority, boredom, and restlessness, and remain chronically uncertain and dissatisfied with themselves (Kernberg 1974). Narcissists have difficulty accepting their real selves and develop false idealized selves that they present to the world in order to get admiration and acceptance (Miller 1981). Furthermore, narcissists only feel valued for successful performances, not for who they really are inside. This is because they make a tragic link between admiration and love (Miller 1981). For example, one very successful narcissistic patient broke her leg. During her recovery she became very depressed, because when she wasn't doing something she felt empty and had little sense of self or of self-worth. To attain self-worth, narcissists are often very ambitious and continually search for brilliance, wealth, power, and beauty (Kernberg 1974). To defend against the deflation of their grandiosity, narcissists tend to distort their perceptions in favor of seeing themselves in a more positive light (Shapiro 1965). This distortion can have tremendous interpersonal consequences.

While narcissists often have a superficially smooth social adaptation, they tend to have serious difficulties in their relationships with other people (Kernberg 1974). They tend to idealize, devalue, and use other people for their functions (e.g., mirroring, admiring, and empathizing) rather than to realistically perceive and relate to them as whole human beings (Johnson 1987). As such, they have serious deficiencies in their ability to love (Kernberg 1974).

Narcissistic Relational Goals and Fantasies

In romantic relationships, the narcissistic personality has several deep-seated wishes, some of them contradictory. The first and most important wish of narcissists is for a selfobject who provides them with the functions that they did not receive to a sufficient degree from their parents in childhood and are thus unable to adequately provide for themselves. Narcissists want to be admired and to be seen, heard and recognized as separate and unique individuals. They wish to be reassured and soothed when they fail or fall upon misfortune. Finally, they want to be understood and accepted for their (albeit imperfect) selves.

The narcissist's second wish is for a partner who in some ways functions as a "slave." Narcissists want someone who will gladly volunteer to take care of the mundane details of their daily lives allowing them greater freedom to develop their special gifts and talents. Narcissists wish for a person that they can completely depend upon to minister to their needs without the person having any needs of his or her own.

Finally, narcissists desire a love object who provides them with a sense of security or stability in their lives. The narcissist wants a partner to be constantly available to reassure him or her of loving continuity. At the same time, the narcissist wants the partner to go away when he or she is otherwise involved. For example, one narcissistic patient frequently traveled on business. When he was in town he expected his wife to be there, drop her plans, and spend every minute with him. When he was on the road, he never called and became angry at his wife's request that he do so. The narcissist thus wishes for a partner who behaves like an ideal "rapprochement" mother (Mahler et al. 1975).

The Narcissistic Personality During Courtship

The narcissistic personality is exceptionally skilled in the art of courtship. Narcissists have had a lifetime of experience of being the idealized objects of significant others in their lives and are highly attuned to the unstated needs, wishes, and fantasies of others (Miller 1981). An example is a narcissistic patient who seduced a man by walking up to him as he was reading outdoors on a hot day and telling him that what he needed was a chocolate ice cream cone (just as he was thinking about one). One narcissistic patient gave a gift to a woman that he was dating consisting of a book of coupons for romantic fantasies (e.g., a trip to Jamaica, a massage, a dinner at a romantic restaurant). While romantic behavior is certainly a component of most courtships, it is carried to an art form by the narcissist.

Furthermore, during courtship, narcissists are often attentive listeners who spend hours seemingly fascinated by hearing the details about their partner's day. They seem sensitive to and appear to understand their partner's innermost emotions. Furthermore, narcissists may express that they most value in their partners that aspect of the partner's self about which he or she is most ashamed. For example, one female patient feared that she was too strong and aggressive for a man to love. She was quite touched during courtship when her narcissistic partner told her that he loved her willfulness.

The narcissist during courtship is a master at seduction. Narcissists often take great pains with their appearance in order to look attractive to their partners. Furthermore, they are skilled in the art of flattery and often make their partners feel attractive and desirable. Finally, they are excellent at soliciting their partner's secret sexual fantasies and overcoming their partner's inhibitions about enacting these fantasies.

THE MASOCHISTIC-NARCISSISTIC COUPLE

The Courtship Phase

The masochistic individual frequently copes with a difficult and often abusive childhood through the development of a rich fantasy life—including romantic fantasies about the ideal partner. Lacking a sufficient basis in experience about what constitutes a realistic, good relationship, the masochist is vulnerable to the larger-than-life promises that the narcissist makes. The narcissist tends to be exceptionally skilled in the art of courtship and thus enacts the masochist's fantasies about ideal partners and ideal love. Due to his or her seeming emotional intensity, the narcissist is able to bypass the masochist's rigid boundaries drawing out the masochist's "hidden child," and meeting his or her unstated and often unconscious dependency needs.

The narcissist is drawn to the masochist's strong, dependable, and confident false self presentation. The masochist initially seems like a capable, giving adult who will take care of the narcissist without needing anything in return. The narcissist hopes that the masochist will provide him or her with a feeling of security. Furthermore, the narcissist initially feels tremendously admired by the masochist and mistakes this for genuine acceptance rather than recognizing this as the type of idealization that occurs during courtship.

Post-Courtship Disillusionment

Following courtship, many couples experience the inevitable disillusionment that occurs as they discover that their partner is different than they had hoped for (Ables and Brandsma 1977). Couples often hope that their partner would be like the parent that they wished for as children. Rather, they frequently find that they have chosen a mate who is a great deal like their parents.

The narcissist initially fulfills the masochist's desire

for idealized symbiosis but later recapitulates the erratic environment of the masochist's childhood (Glickauf-Hughes and Wells 1991). Masochists often discover, to their dismay, that their partners are in many ways like their narcissistic parents. The person who previously seemed so loving, tender, and romantic now seems critical, rejecting, and/or abusive. Like the masochist's parents, the narcissist has a tendency to use projection and projective identification. They thus tend to view relational difficulties as primarily the masochist's fault.

Although the relationship becomes painful and de-priving for masochists, they tend to persevere due to their fear of loss and use of introjection. Masochists believe (as they did with their parents) that their partner has all the needed supplies and that if only they could determine the right thing to do, their partner would be giving to them in the way that they want and need. This belief is reinforced by the intermittent, intensely positive gratification given by the narcissist, which leaves the masochist believing that the narcissist's love is potentially available and that he or she has some control over attaining it. For example, one client's partner stopped calling him for two weeks and then sent him an extravagant gift with a loving note.

Narcissists, on the other hand, initially believe that, unlike their parents, they have finally found a giving, unselfish individual who loves and accepts them for their true self. Following courtship, the narcissist discovers that while the masochist behaves in a generous manner, he or she is often giving to get something in return. Further-more, masochists' difficulty in stating their needs directly, combined with their desire to remain in a dominant position, can make them behave in ways that the narcissist experiences as controlling and manipulative. When the narcissist confronts the masochist about his or her controlling and/or passive-aggressive behavior, the masochist often uses denial (as the narcissist's parents did), causing the narcissist to feel like the angry one in the relationship. The most disappointing thing that narcissists discover after courtship is that while they had hoped that they were being accepted by the masochist for their real selves, that acceptance seems to be contingent upon their continuing to behave in an ideal manner as they did during courtship.

Thus, after courtship, when both partners start to behave more authentically (and behave at times in a manner that replicates each individual's family of origin), each person begins to develop a transference reaction to their partner. In both cases, the transference reaction is to some extent an accurate representation of the other and to some extent a distortion from the past. The narcissist begins to see the masochist as an engulfing, dependent, fragile parent who suppresses and controls his or her real self. The masochist sees the narcissist as an exciting and rejecting object who alternates between being seductive, charming, and loving, and being abusive and rejecting. The masochist experiences him- or herself as being locked in an old pattern of loving an object who gives nonlove in return.

Couples Dynamics

Both the narcissist and the masochist suffer from disorders of the self (Horner 1979) and use one another to try to gain the functions that they are unable to provide for themselves (e.g., security, self-soothing, self-esteem). Furthermore, in many areas the narcissist and the masochist have complementary issues that cause them to become entangled in different circular patterns with one another. Both of these factors contribute to their having a high degree of enmeshment in their relationship. One aspect of this complementarily is that narcissists tend to project unwanted aspects of themselves onto others, whereas masochists have a propensity to introject or internalize aspects of others that aren't really a part of them. For example, a narcissist wife (who was unable to accept her own feelings of fear) told her masochistic husband that she thought he wasn't successful enough due to his anxiety and difficulty taking risks. While the masochistic husband was in fact far more successful and risk-taking than his wife, he still took her accusations to heart.

While masochists do not use projection and projective identification as a common defense, they do use it at times around the experience of anger. Masochists experience great guilt and shame when they experience anger toward their partners and fear that it will result in the demise of the relationship (Menaker 1953). They may defend against this fear by attributing their angry feelings to their partner. At times they may even behave in ways (e.g., passive-aggressiveness) that induce angry feelings in their partner.

While narcissists tend to be comfortable with their angry feelings, they feel great shame and discomfort about their dependency needs and their feelings of fear, depression, and shame (Kernberg 1976). They thus tend to attribute these feelings to the masochistic partner and in fact behave toward the masochist in ways that actually induce these feelings. By chronically rejecting the masochist, the narcissist increases the masochist's dependency needs. By behaving in a critical and angry manner toward the masochist, the narcissist exacerbates the masochist's feelings of shame. By repeatedly threatening to abandon the masochist, the narcissist intensifies the masochist's preexisting fears of separation. These behaviors collectively may contribute to the masochist's feelings of depression.

Another area where the narcissist and masochist have opposite but complementary issues is the optimal amount of distance in the relationship. The masochist fears abandonment whereas the narcissist fears engulfment. Narcissists experience the masochist as engulfing and protect themselves by withdrawal. Masochists experience the narcissist as rejecting and attempt to stave off potential abandonment by clinging to their partner. The more that the masochist clings, the more that the narcissist withdraws. The more that the narcissist withdraws, the more the masochist clings. Both believe that their behavior is caused by the other.

Another polarized but complementary area for the couple centers around responsibility and control. The masochist tends to be overresponsible and controlling, whereas the narcissist (in a further attempt to resist engulfment) tends to be irresponsible and rebellious. Narcissists believe that they are rebelling because their partners are so controlling. Masochists believe that they are so controlling because their partners are so irresponsible. Willi (1982) refers to this couples pattern as an "anal-sadistic collusion."

Another important but troublesome distinction between the partners in this type of relationship is that the masochist tends to have boundaries that are too rigid, whereas the narcissist frequently has boundaries that are too loose. While this difference initially draws the couple to each other, it ultimately creates friction in the relationship. Narcissists tend to push limits and masochists have difficulty setting them. For example, a narcissistic husband frequently wished to have sex with his wife late at night (although she needed to get up early in the morning for work). The masochistic wife was unable to say no to him. She resentfully stayed up to have sex but was unresponsive. The husband (in hopes of getting his wife to respond) tried to get her to stay up even later.

Another problem area for the couple is that the masochist and narcissist have different bottom-line issues. The masochist is willing to sacrifice self-esteem to keep the relationship, whereas the narcissist is willing to sacrifice the relationship for power and self-esteem. Thus in arguments with one another, the masochist becomes so frightened about losing the relationship that he or she tends to apologize first and accepts more than his or her share of responsibility for relational difficulties. Admitting culpability about relational problems fills narcissists with such shame that they often withdraw during arguments and rarely apologize.

Psychotherapy of the Masochistic-Narcissistic Couple

As the problems of the masochistic-narcissistic pair occur at both an individual and a relational level, treatment for this couple must deal with issues at both the intrapsychic and interpersonal levels. As such, psychotherapy must address treatment issues of both the masochistic and the narcissistic partner. Treatment must also be designed to help solve problems arising from the particular interaction of both personality types in relationship with one another.

To review, some previously stated treatment goals for the masochistic individual are as follows. It is important to help the masochist learn to ask that his or her dependency needs be met directly, rather than vicariously through taking care of others. This involves helping the masochist to develop an awareness of what he or she needs and the ability to ask that the needs be met in a manner that assures they are. Masochists are so ashamed of their needs and mistrustful of others that when they do ask that needs be met, they tend to do so in a hostile or guilt-inducing manner that alienates others (e.g., "You probably don't really want to help me but . . . "). Furthermore, masochists must learn to receive what is given. They need to learn to temporarily give up control and be vulnerable by choice—not just as a result of being abused or broken down in a conflict. Masochists must also learn to be more assertive, developing both the ability to say no to others and the ability to express anger appropriately. They must be taught to fight like an adult—neither behaving in a passive-aggressive manner nor losing their temper. Masochists also need help in strengthening their fragile sense of self-esteem and tenuous ability to empathize with themselves. This includes their learning to develop and pursue goals that reflect their own ideal self rather than living vicariously through the accomplishments of their narcissistic partner. Masochists must be helped to establish object constancy so that they become more able to endure separations and loss.

Treatment goals for the narcissistic individual are as follows. Most important is to help the narcissist to develop a sense of self (Johnson 1987). Narcissistic individuals need to know who they are and what they want rather than only being and doing (or not doing) what their parents or partners want. This includes learning to experience and accept the unwanted aspects of themselves that they tend to fragment off (Horner 1979) and project onto their partners (e.g., dependency, sadness, and fear). The narcissist must also give up his or her grandiose goals and ideals and replace them with more realistic ones. The narcissist must be helped to work through the defense of splitting and to see and accept others as both good and bad at the same time (Masterson 1981). The development of object constancy significantly improves the narcissist's ability to fight without becoming enraged.

In working with narcissistic and masochistic individuals in couples therapy, there are several important couple's goals to be addressed. Most important of these is to help the couple become less enmeshed with one another. When they discuss arguments with each other in the couple's therapy session, it is important to help both partners to (a) unravel the difficulties that they get into with each other and (b) accept without blame their own needs, feelings, and behaviors. As they are helped individually to accept unwanted aspects of themselves and to develop firm but flexible boundaries, they can be helped as a couple to identify when they are using projection and introjection with one another. Both the narcissist and the masochist need to learn to take more responsibility for their needs, feelings, and behaviors. Another way that the couple can become more separate is for both partners to learn to depend more on other people outside the primary relationship.

Part of learning to assume responsibility for oneself is learning to responsibly address one's dependency needs and feelings of anger. Narcissists tend to hint about what they need and masochists tend to get their dependency needs met vicariously. Both must learn to ask for things more directly. With regard to anger, narcissists tend to become enraged and masochists tend to behave passive-aggressively. Both need to learn to express their angry feelings as one adult to another, maintaining at all times the part of themselves that is a friendly observer.

Both the narcissist and the masochist need to develop realistic goals for both themselves and their relationships.

They must learn that people and relationships are neither wonderful nor horrible. As part of this process, they need help in grieving their lost relational dreams and ideals. However, while they need to give up the hope of attaining the prince or princess of their dreams, they open the potential of developing a loving, sexual friendship with a partner that they have come to trust.

Pitfalls in Psychotherapy with the Masochistic-Narcissistic Couple

In working with masochistic-narcissistic couples, there are several dangerous pitfalls that the therapist must try to avoid: (a) reforming the narcissist, (b) creating identified patients, and (c) "masochistic triangulation" (Horner 1979).

In psychotherapy of the masochistic-narcissistic couple (where the masochist does 80 percent of the giving in the relationship and the narcissist does 20 percent of the giving), it is the natural tendency of therapists to place greater emphasis upon attempting to get narcissists to be more generous with their partners. This tends to be a no-win strategy that inspires shame and resistance in the narcissist and leaves both members of the couple feeling discouraged. A more useful approach is to encourage the masochist to be less giving and to learn to take better care of him- or herself. While this approach may inspire some resistance in the masochist (as it goes against his or her ego ideal), it has a greater probability of a successful outcome.

The second pitfall to avoid in working with the masochistic-narcissistic couple is making either partner the identified patient. The masochist who comes into therapy looking very depressed and having suicidal ideation runs the risk of being regarded as the sick patient. Due to the narcissist's fear of engulfment and vigilance against being coerced into false self behavior, he or she may behave in therapy in what appears to be a resistant, uncooperative, and seemingly selfish manner and runs the risk of being regarded as the bad patient. A helpful strategy is to view the masochist as carrying the couple's sadness and the narcissist as carrying the couple's aggression and self-protectiveness and to discuss with the couple the importance of distributing these roles more evenly between them.

The final and perhaps most dangerous pitfall that therapists encounter in working with the masochistic-narcissistic couple is the phenomenon of "masochistic triangulation" described earlier in the book (Horner 1979). To review this process, in masochistic triangulation, the masochistic patient, acts out an intrapsychic split between his or her good and bad internal objects within the context of a triangle. This acting out requires three people: (a) the bad, persecutory object (the narcissist); (b) the good, rescuing object (the therapist); and (c) the good self or victim (the masochist). The good, rescuing object has several functions in this triangle: (a) containing the masochist's rage to protect the masochist from experiencing it (and thus becoming the bad self), and (b) validating the masochist's anger so that it feels morally justified. Having the hate expressed and externalized in the therapist, the masochist then only experiences his or her positive, loving feelings for the narcissistic partner.

At this point, however, having contained the masochist's rage the therapist may feel propelled to urge the masochist to break off the relationship with the narcissistic or may grow frustrated with the masochistic patient for not making any changes. The expression of either impulse is a grave therapeutic error. Rather, the therapist must help masochists own their anger and rage and integrate it with their loving feelings for their partner. The therapist must also help the masochistic patient to see how triangles occur that really externalize a conflict that is within him- or herself.

In summary, we have reviewed the salient character- istics of narcissistic and masochistic personalities, in- cluding their relational goals and fantasies. The behavioral patterns of the masochistic-narcissistic couple during and following courtship were then traced, including their ten- dency to have polarized traits that greatly entangle them with one another. Finally, specific treatment goals and strategies were recommended, as well as particular pitfalls that must be avoided. In the next chapter, treatment goals and strategies for masochistic patients in group therapy will be addressed.

13

Treating Masochistic Personalities in Object Relations/ Interactional Group Psychotherapy

Group psychotherapy often serves as either an effective primary treatment format or as a vital adjunct therapy for masochistic personalities, given their relational focus and interpersonal difficulties. In addition, masochistic dynamics are common among group patients with a mixed personality diagnosis who meet some but not all of the prerequisite criteria for diagnosis as a masochistic personality.

Masochistic personalities usually enter therapy because their relationships are unsatisfying and painful. In typical fashion, masochistic patients often begin treatment complaining that they are being mistreated in their intimate relationships and suspect that this is because there is something wrong with them. They thus tend to be quite motivated for a therapeutic experience, which can help them understand and learn how to change their interpersonal patterns in a safe and supportive environment with others.

As a result, therapists who lead groups may commonly observe patients who use masochistic triangulation or masochistic splitting, exhibit a pattern of help-rejecting complaining, and/or present as a chronic helper. Therapists thus are well advised to train themselves in group treatment of this clinical population. However, we recently searched the psychology literature and found, surprisingly, only one publication that explored group treatment of patients with masochistic dynamics (Light 1974) and none on group therapy of patients diagnosed as masochistic or self-defeating.

This chapter describes the treatment of masochistic personalities in an object relations/interactional group therapy paradigm, and discusses (a) the group model under consideration, (b) the specific advantages of group therapy for masochistic personalities, (c) the therapeutic goals for this personality organization, and (d) various object relations–based treatment strategies aimed at both increasing the patient's insight and providing corrective relationship experiences. Finally, we examine how the masochistic personality typically interacts with other personalities in group and how clinicians can therapeutically use these interactions as well as their own countertransference responses to maximize the masochistic patient's interpersonal and intrapsychic healing.

OBJECT RELATIONS/INTERACTIVE GROUP TREATMENT

The object relations/interactional group therapy paradigm represents a variation of the dynamic interactional model described by Yalom (1975). We originally referred to this model as an interpersonal-psychodynamic model of group therapy (Wells et al. 1990).

Briefly, this model is based on the principles of object relations therapy and is conducted in an interactional format that includes a mixture of (a) stimulating group interaction and feedback, (b) group interpretation, and (c) individual patient focus as needed. Because object relations theories focus on the internalization of significant relationships and on corrective relationship experiences, group therapy holds special potential for understanding a person's intrapsychic template and for fostering healing interpersonal experiences.

Since object relations therapy purports that individuals' psychic templates are reflected in the quality and pattern of their interpersonal relationships, psychotherapy groups afford an *in vivo* opportunity for the therapist to understand patients' mental mapping by studying the patterns of interpersonal interactions and relationships that are formed with the group leader and other group members. According to Ganzarain (1992), object relations group psychotherapy "focuses on the internal fantasied world of psychic reality, more specifically on the exchanges between the self and the internal images of others, or mental residues of their relations with the self" (p. 205). The little that has been published in the literature on object relations group therapy has focused on the treatment of more severe character disorders and thus stresses intrapsychic functioning and group-level interpretations and interventions. Object relations/interactional therapy is a treatment format that can readily be expanded to facilitate preneurotic and neurotic as well as borderline-level character disorders.

In fact, it is recommended that borderline-level patients be excluded from treatment groups with preneurotic- and neurotic-level patients for a variety of reasons. Yalom (1970) excludes more severely disturbed patients because, with their use of primitive splitting and projective identifications, these patients frequently fail to successfully integrate themselves into the communication and relationship network of the group. These relationship patterns can lead to hostility and scapegoating or unproductive passivity by the group, thus significantly impeding the development of a cohesive working group.

The authors also recommend that these psychotherapy groups include patients with different character organizations so that various *in vivo* patterns of interaction will be stimulated and available for analysis. It is often helpful to include more than one masochistic patient, however, so that the masochist can observe another individual's masochistic behavior patterns. This treatment format potentially fosters more objectivity and affords opportunities for strengthening observing ego functions. In this manner, masochistic patients can help each other by providing understanding from one's own experience as well as emotional support during the process of examining self-defeating relationship patterns.

It is also recommended that these groups include one or two more hostile-dominant personalities (Benjamin 1993, Leary 1975) because of their stimulus value to the masochistic patient. Masochists typically were raised in a narcissistic and/or hostile-dominant family environment and learned their favored survival patterns of intimacy within that context. As a result, they are often drawn to recapitulate family dynamics with hostile-dominant individuals (e.g., narcissistic, sadistic), which can generate opportunities for greater understanding and change.

The object relations/interactional model of group therapy has two major premises. The first premise is that character structures develop partly through evolving autonomous functions and partly through evolving relationships with other individuals. Modification of character style, including associated structural defects, thus re-

quires corrective relationship experiences. Group psychotherapy can be especially effective in providing a variety of
effective corrective relationship experiences. For example,
with obsessive-compulsive personalities who are generally
overcontrolled and constricted in their affective expression,
group therapy can afford an evocative interpersonal experience for obsessives to respond to as well as *in vivo*
demonstrations of what they are missing out on by their
dedication to self-control and being right (Wells et al.
1990). For masochistic personalities who are generally
prone to assuming either a caretaking or victim stance,
group psychotherapy can illuminate for these individuals
(a) how uncomfortable they are receiving what they believe
they want (e.g., compliments, nurturing), (b) how they
tend to overfocus on what they complain about (e.g.,
criticism, rejection, non-love), and (c) how they tend to
insist on winning love and approval from individuals who
are rejecting and nonreciprocal with them.

The second premise is that individuals' unresolved
current and past developmental issues (e.g., attachment,
basic trust, separation-individuation, autonomy, initiative,
identity, intimacy) often interfere with their interpersonal
relationships. These unresolved issues tend to propel
group members into re-creating with one another the
self-defeating relationship patterns that have been shaped
by their developmental history and that they experience in
their everyday lives. For masochists, this re-creation is
often developed through mechanisms such as projective
identification, masochistic splitting, and help-rejecting
complaining.

The therapy group can thus provide an individual
with both awareness and insight into his or her character
style, including both its strengths and deficits. Furthermore, opportunities (treatment strategies) can be structured by the group therapist to help patients work through

developmental tasks and learn more adaptive interpersonal behaviors that can ultimately lead to the modification of character style. The object relations/interactional model of group psychotherapy thus attempts to increase the patient's insight into underlying motivations as well as provide the patient with a corrective interpersonal experience that addresses early deficits. Group therapy potentially facilitates insight by providing a safe and supportive place to observe developing relationships as well as providing a variety of personalities or cast of characters as potential transference objects. Therapy groups also potentially offer more opportunities for corrective experiences from the therapist and group members, and a great deal of feedback that can provide patients with a variety of different perspectives and opportunities to practice new ways of relating to others.

We agree with Selwyn (1988) that the group therapy setting reflects a family structure of parental and sibling roles that fosters individual and group projections of idealizing and critial superego transferences onto the group, therapist, and fellow members. Psychotherapy groups thus provide an almost ideal setting for the stimulation of masochism as a defense against projected superego aggression as well as striving for security attachments.

ADVANTAGES OF GROUP FORMAT FOR THE MASOCHISTIC PATIENT

When character traits are ego-syntonic and the patient's observing ego is entangled in personality traits and defenses, group feedback in a respectful, empathic, honest atmosphere often has more impact than individual psychotherapy. For example, more than one person offering feedback over time can help to challenge a patient's defenses such as denial, minimalization, and rationalization. Such defenses often protect the patient from allowing the individual therapist's interpretations to influence them. Character neurotics frequently do not realize how the traits they value so highly are largely responsible for the tensions they experience with others and within themselves (Peck 1978). Masochists, in particular, believe that the world needs more altruistic and self-sacrificing people. They do not enter treatment stating that they want to be less holier-than-thou or learn how to get more comfortable receiving from others. In fact, they often think the problem is that they need to give even more to others than they already do.

For example, one patient described a long-standing relationship with his brother that was very painful. His brother generally told jokes at the patient's expense, interrupted the patient when they were in conversation with others, told the patient that he was stupid whenever they disagreed, and accused the patient of "being a baby" or "being too sensitive, like a girl" when the patient complained. When this patient entered therapy he pleaded with the therapist for assistance, noting, "If only I could be a better person and learn how not to get so frustrated or angry with him and learn to forgive faster, I think my relationship with my brother would be so much better and I wouldn't feel so miserable with him all the time."

Group psychotherapists can thus help patients see the disadvantages of rigid role assumptions. With masochistic patients, in particular, groups can elucidate the problem of chronically assuming a caretaking or victim role. For example, when individuals predominantly assume such a role, they tend to miss out on getting taken care of themselves. One patient, who clearly complained about the general lack of nurturance in her relationships, found herself nevertheless discounting compliments or statements of appreciation offered by other group members. When the therapist pointed out how she was training the group not to compliment her, she cried in sadness about her lost opportunities.

Given that the caretaking role is so ego-syntonic, psychotherapy groups are often especially helpful in demonstrating to patients *in vivo* how they experience discomfort receiving what they request from others (e.g., appreciation, compliments, nurturing) and thus consequently overfocus on what they complain about (e.g., criticism, rejection, non-love). In the example cited above, the patient not only shrugged off all compliments, but she also overfocused on what she was not able to get with particular hostile-dominant group members. She especially wanted the approval of a bright, articulate, narcissistic group member who did not consider her "cool enough to bother with" because she was overweight and relatively needy. He found her solicitations too demanding and intrusive and usually responded to her with hostility before their interactions were over. The masochistic patient would then complain about how unsatisfying her relationships were. She would assert that "the world seemed like a stingy and selfish place where everyone was out for themselves and you had to be perfect to get any attention." When the therapist would point out how she tried so hard to get her needs met with someone who felt put off by her advances, while she seemed to undervalue all the support other people genuinely felt for her, she said that she experienced the others as just telling her what they thought she wanted to hear to falsely cheer her up while she could count on the discriminating taste and painful honesty of the narcissistic group member.

Psychotherapy groups can also offer an especially helpful format for giving masochistic patients feedback about the "red flags" that these patients often overlook in conflictual relationships. Masochistic patients are particularly practiced at denying the signs that foretell of difficulties to come. When faced with interpersonal difficulties, many masochistic patients combine cognitive fog or dissociative reactions with denial. As a result they have difficulty remembering the details about problematic interactions with significant others. Group members can help the patient reconstruct painful interactions and learn to recognize the warning signals or "red flags" by sharing their own observations and telling stories about their own internal "red flag reactions." By asking patients how they feel at critical moments of engagement, masochistic patients can learn to identify their own internal signals and use them informationally to learn alternative ways of interacting that are more conscious and less reactive.

Groups can also demonstrate for masochistic patients how they set up help-rejecting–complaining interactions. For example, a patient may describe a problem situation in an urgent or depressed tone and then say, "I don't know what to do." Group members often feel the implied invitation to help and respond by giving the indirectly solicited advice rather than empathy. The patient then proceeds to frustrate group members by either directly or subtly resisting everyone's suggestions. The patient's resistance sometimes reflects self-defeating attempts at striving for individuation. The sequence can also represent the behavioral-induction phase of projective identification. This pattern can also reflect the masochistic patients' lack of knowledge about what they really need or want coupled with their discomfort in directly asking and actually receiving it.

Group interactions can demonstrate how masochistic patients can project internal objects onto others and trigger behavioral responses in others of being persecutors or rescuers (Ganzarain 1992). One masochistic patient who struggled with a painful attachment to her husband repeatedly described to the group in a tearful manner how she felt mistreated. Most group members initially responded by sympathizing with this patient, becoming angry with her husband, and encouraging her to take better care of herself. One more schizoid group member, however, often remained silent and disengaged while this patient was talking. When the therapist asked this masochistic patient how she felt with the group, she said she was anxious because the more schizoid group member was very quiet. When asked what she imagined he was thinking or feeling, the patient said he seemed to feel critical of her. She imagined he felt disgusted with her weakness and her whining and was irritated with her for taking up so much group time. The schizoid group member had become the transferential manifestations of the masochistic patient's contemptuous father, who sarcastically devalued her mother whenever she complained about something.

INTERPERSONAL TREATMENT GOALS WITH MASOCHISTIC PATIENTS

In this group-treatment model therapeutic goals are aimed at both interpersonal and intrapsychic change. The interpersonal goals are discussed in the following subsections.

Chronic Patterns

An important goal is to help the patient recognize, understand, and resolve any chronic pattern of assuming the caretaker–victim role, and the accompanying dynamic issues (Light 1974). The patient is encouraged to identify and practice alternative, healthier patterns of moderate altruism and appropriate self-interest. For some masochistic patients this goal may also include helping them to see how they induce narcissistic mirroring in individuals with similar dynamics. In one therapy group two masochistic patients developed a competitive pattern of trying to be the most helpful and thus the most "special" patient to the leader and other group members. Each patient needed to understand how he or she gave things to others with strings attached, or gave in order to get. They also needed to understand how old family sibling rivalries were being reenacted as they subtly competed with each other. When these masochistic patients did not feel sufficiently appreciated or treated reciprocally in precisely the way they wanted to be, one patient tended to cry while the other tended to pout (indirectly expressing their anger and outrage). Group members began to feel blackmailed by these patients and finally expressed resentment about their conditional giving.

Masochistic patients often feel hurt and shamed by this feedback. Because of their histories, they can confuse feeling hurt and shamed with being punished or abused. Masochistic patients often believe that they must hide their hurt and shame from others, believing that they need to rise above such emotions and feeling ashamed of their vulnerability. It is thus often important for the group therapist to help the masochistic patient to feel safe and supported enough to acknowledge feeling hurt and punished by group members who give them negative feedback. As one patient noted, "I try so hard to please everyone and be a good person. It just doesn't seem fair that people come down on me for wanting a little support in return. When Joe said he felt blackmailed by me, I just wanted to die. It felt so humiliating. I wish I'd never let anyone know what I want as I just seem to get punished for it."

In this scenario, someone has to be a "bad person"– either the group member who shared the negative feedback or the patient for being needy. The group therapist thus needs to help the masochistic patient and the other group members sort out hurt feelings from actual abuse or sadistic behavior. Both patient and group members need to understand the way in which shame can link hurt and perceived punishment and the masochist's tendency in ambiguous situations to manifest a narcissistic transference and thus perceive others as selfish, cold, and critical. In an ambiguous situation, when the masochistic patient does not know the real intent of the group member who gave the feedback, he or she may find it difficult to give people the benefit of the doubt. Helping the patient to ask for clarification can begin a dialogue that has the potential to repair the felt rift between the masochistic patient and other group members.

Although it is often difficult for group members to give and for masochistic patients to receive such feedback, it can be extremely helpful to masochistic patients in increasing their awareness of the impact of their behavior on others. In addition, an opportunity is often created for the masochist to practice giving more moderately in order to allow more room for others to reciprocate. Other group members may be asked to help this patient to set reasonable limits on giving. To experiment with giving more moderately, the masochist may also need to learn to trust that others will do what needs to be done if they do not volunteer. Sometimes, asking the masochistic patient which group members, in particular, he or she does not trust may help to concretize and personalize the masochist's more global and diffuse feelings and beliefs.

A dialogue between the two group members may help the patient to clarify the transferential component of these feelings and beliefs and develop an explicitly stated and mutually agreed upon way of handling these situations. When one masochistic patient gets into an impasse with the group, it can be helpful for the therapist to ask a second masochistic patient to help the group and the patient to better understand the feelings of insecurity and the desperate need for consistent reassurance of lovability and basic acceptability that frequently motivate the masochist's behavior.

Masochistic individuals also need to learn that they can develop more satisfying relationships with others by keeping their own wishes, needs, and preferences in the equation. Therapy groups can provide masochistic patients with multiple opportunities to witness other patients appropriately expressing their needs and getting these needs met by other people.

Masochistic patients tend to believe that they must set their own needs aside in order to sustain relationships, in large measure due to their shame over feeling needy and thus weak. They often believe that to be vulnerable is to put oneself at risk of humiliation. Avoidance of shame over potential exposure is particularly activated in groups where many witnesses and potential judges are present.

Masochistic patients often need to increase their awareness of how they tend to withdraw from others and avoid acknowledging their needs in order to manage shame. Observing when these patients look away and encouraging them to maintain eye contact in order to remain aware of their feelings and needs can be helpful in overcoming shame and consequent avoidance mechanisms that frustrate the patient's psychological growth.

In one of the authors' groups, a masochistic patient initially presented herself as a junior therapist, proceeding to assist other group members with their problems to the best of her ability. The patient had served as her family's mediator and "pseudotherapist" and then extended this role into a career as a master's-level graduate student in psychiatric nursing. When the group eventually expressed concern that she was always helping others and never talked about her own concerns, this patient said that she just was not quite ready to get into her "stuff." When some group members expressed discomfort about her over-containment, she became visibly uncomfortable and indirectly let the group know she felt criticized and unappreciated. The group then backed off and let her do her "thing," causing her to feel rejected and ignored.

The second critical opportunity arose for this patient when she decided to be vulnerable and began telling the group in detail about a painful incident, periodically noting that she "didn't know what to do." While this statement appeared to invite advice, her story indicated that she had indeed thought of almost every option and had found a reason why that option was not viable. The group, eager to be helpful to her, began giving her their best advice anyway. Frustration among group members began to mount when the patient found something wrong with each offering. She noted that, "I've already tried that," or "That won't work because . . . " At no point did she acknowledge the intended or potential helpfulness of their suggestions. Determined to be helpful and giving, members continued to try to find solutions to the problems that she shared. When the therapist asked both the patient and the group members how they felt, all were frustrated. The patient, however, was also eventually able to acknowledge some satisfaction in having thought of everything that all the group members brought up and in being able to "document how it wouldn't work." For this patient, this activity was especially satisfying because it kept others involved with her in a manner in which she could avoid real vulnerability and avoid being seen by others as inadequate.

At another level, through projective identification, the transactions also induced the group, who now represented her bad, pre-oedipal mother, to experience for themselves just how inept her mother really was at parenting. The group was thus induced by this patient's help-rejecting behavior into experiencing feelings of inadequacy and ineffectualness.

The patient's biological father had left the family when the patient was 4. The mother, in a state of helpless frustration, loneliness, and insecurity, often overconfided in her young daughter, who quickly learned to listen to and contain her mother's feelings. The mother remarried when the patient was 6; the new husband was an alcoholic. The new family unit moved every other year to accommodate her stepfather's alcohol-related difficulties at work. The patient assumed more and more adult functioning to care for her mother. Her stepfather would "tear into" her whenever he saw any chink in her armor, so it was important to behave in a manner that was above reproach. In her help-rejecting behaviors with the group, this patient thus managed to induce feelings of maternal ineptness in group members while remaining above reproach herself. Her behavior thus represented an identification with her stepfather, in which she felt the power of commanding assistance and then judging its adequacy, telling others how they were wrong or inept.

Over time, with the assistance of the therapist and feedback from the group, this patient gradually became aware of this pattern and began to relate it to relationship patterns that she experienced outside of group. With the therapist's assistance, a contract was negotiated between the patient and the group that included (a) the patient's agreement to work on directly telling the group when she felt needy and insecure and wanted attention and understanding (rather than advice), and (b) the group's agreement to empathize with the patient rather than offering her advice or suggestions unless they were explicitly invited to do so by the patient. Through such new experiences, over time, masochistic patients may learn to trust the safe, relatively consistent and supportive environment of the group. They may also learn to metacommunicate or editorialize at those times when they feel compelled to engage others indirectly.

Ambivalent or Anxious Attachment

Another goal of therapy is to help the patient recognize, understand, and resolve related ambivalent or anxious attachment, especially to individuals who are more rejecting and nonreciprocal with them. Masochistic patients need practice in relating to individuals who are more naturally giving. In addition, they must learn to invest self-esteem in self-development and self-in-relationship with safe and supportive others as opposed to relationships with mostly rejecting and nongiving others.

One way in which therapists can facilitate masochistic patients' recognition of special attachments to rejecting objects is to clarify instances in which the patient solicits support from critical group members and discounts support from noncritical group members. The historical roots and meaning of these inclinations need to be truly understood and appreciated. For example, this pattern in one masochistic patient represented an attempt to win the approval of a critical and mostly absent father in order to be worthy of his love and acceptance. Once this patient felt understood and accepted by the group for these strivings, the group was able to help him learn to become more comfortable receiving support from group members who were not critical of him.

Separation and Loss

When loss becomes less threatening for patients, they have more options. Patients need help in identifying pathological mourning and practicing healthy grieving. Part of this process involves the use of the group as a secure, transitional space that they can count on to be there, even if relationships in their life change. The group helped one masochistic patient feel more secure in the world by serving as the first safe, good-enough, reasonably predictable "family" experience that she had ever known.

Learning to Genuinely Depend on Others

It is important to help masochists (a) become more aware of their dependency needs, (b) express their needs more appropriately, and (c) become a good receiver. When one masochistic patient was complaining about a series of problems that she was having and the therapist noticed that the group members manifested subtle signs of impatience, the therapist helped the masochistic patient to understand and directly ask for what she was needing from the group at that moment and why she was afraid to ask for it. In this instance, the patient experienced the group as he had experienced his mother (as an exciting and rejecting object). Whenever she promised him something that he needed, she eventually disappointed him. This patient thus learned to believe that if he didn't feel or express needs, he wouldn't be disappointed.

Assertiveness

Group therapy can increase patients' comfort with assertiveness including direct expressions of feelings and needs. Due to their shame about needs and feelings, masochistic patients often have great difficulty expressing them directly. For example, one patient had a tendency to change the subject every time someone asked her a question that made her uncomfortable. In noting and understanding this pattern, the therapist helped her instead to tell the group that she would "prefer not to answer that question right now but would rather think about it first." As in the film *Annie Hall*, masochistic patients need help in expressing the "subtitles" that reflect their real thoughts and feelings.

INTRAPSYCHIC GOALS WITH THE MASOCHISTIC PATIENT

The intrapsychic goals in this group treatment model center around helping patients (a) develop transmuting internalizations for genuine, reality-based self-soothing and self-esteem, including helping them understand how they resist internalizing the empathy of group members because they feel ashamed and undeserving (Jordan 1993); (b) recognize and resolve "masochistic splitting" (Meyers, 1988); (c) strengthen their observing ego by asking them to editorialize on their interactions and internal processing (i.e., help them to articulate what has been private and put words to what has been expressed through actions rather than words); (d) grieve idealized fantasies of self and others (Glickauf-Hughes and Wells in press); and (e) better understand their intractable painful attachments. Examples of how to accomplish these treatment goals are given in Chapter 8.

OBJECT RELATIONS-BASED GROUP TREATMENT WITH MASOCHISTIC PATIENTS

Providing Patients with Corrective Relationship Experience

The group therapist needs to help create a group atmosphere of respect and regard, to notice self-defeating relationship patterns, and to help patients take advantage of opportunities for corrective experiences as they occur. To create a facilitative atmosphere in individual therapy, the therapist is generally advised to (a) be empathic and demonstrate genuine positive regard for patient; (b) be constant, dependable, reliable, and nonreactive, especially when they catastrophize; (c) acknowledge relational mistakes and empathic failures without undue apologies; (d) be emotionally available without being possessive, controlling, or infantilizing; and (e) actively support the patient's efforts at autonomous selfhood (e.g., when masochistic patients manifest resistance, recognize that it is often important for these patients to say "no" before saying "yes" to others).

In addition to the above guidelines outlined more fully in Chapters 7 and 8 on the individual treatment of masochistic personalities, several guidelines specifically for group treatment formats are particularly relevant. For example, to facilitate a reparative group atmosphere where the masochistic patient can learn to trust others enough to risk being vulnerable, the therapist must first be concerned with developing sufficient safety for these patients. This safety can be addressed at different levels. At the group level, group rules, boundaries, and contracts can help to establish a general atmosphere of safety. Issues such as confidentiality, physical acting out, coming to the group under the influence of drugs or alcohol, and each member's expected time commitment (e.g., six months) need to be discussed and agreed upon at the group's inception so that patients know what they can count on from the therapist and from one another.

At an individual patient level, safety can be enhanced by encouraging group members to set good limits for themselves and to develop internal safe or quiet places through visualization. At the interpersonal level, patients may make contracts with one another to be each other's ally or advisor. For example, one masochistic group member was asked to choose another member to serve as her "big sibling" in the group to help her set good limits for herself when she needed help. Many masochists have had their personal boundaries (psychological and physical) repeatedly violated by significant others and thus may need more attention paid to this issue than other patients.

In addition, therapists can facilitate the development of a reparative group environment by modeling some of the behaviors that group members will eventually assume. For example, the therapist will observe patterns of interaction between group members and then ask for reactions or offer a group interpretation intended to further group discussion of a particular group issue, like trust, intimacy, or control.

With masochistic patients therapists may watch for

particular patterns, such as some masochists' tendency to initially give only positive feedback to others as they believe that they should like everyone and very much want everyone to like them. In this case, the therapist might model both self-reflectiveness and directness by observing with the patient that only positive comments were made and wondering what that may mean for the patient. The therapist may inquire about what other group members think of this practice? Masochists generally have a difficult time giving honest feedback to others because of the sensitivity to criticism that they project onto others. Their style of relating is generally designed to protect others from the direct expression of their anger in order to avoid jeopardizing the relationship. Masochists often literally do not know and thus need to experience how criticism and anger can be expressed constructively and used informatively to clear the air and help make future decisions. The therapist can either underscore another group member's constructive criticism, asking the recipient how it felt to hear what was said and what was helpful about it, or the therapist can model this activity and then process it with the group.

Providing Insight about Relevant Issues

In addition to providing corrective relationship experiences, therapists are advised to help masochistic patients develop insight about (a) intractable attachments to predominantly critical and rejecting love objects, (b) their tendency toward overdetermined caretaking, (c) their propensity to unconsciously frustrate other people, (d) narcissistic transferences, (e) resistances to being dependent, and (f) masochistic splitting and triangulation. Therapists may help patients to become aware of the existence, origin, and dynamic function of the patterns as they occur in the group and to relate them to outside relational problems.

Countertransference Reactions: Indications of Family Recapitulations

Group is a ready environment for the reenactment of family dynamics, given the parallel positions of parents (or group leaders) and siblings (group members). Stimulus cues thus often evoke transference and countertransference feelings in the group members as well as in the therapists. This situation provides many opportunities for understanding what is not being said as well as what is.

Having co-therapists can often be of great help in understanding countertransference-evoking situations as one therapist can remain more disengaged and objective while the other one engages the group and allows his or her countertransference feelings to emerge. Therapists can thus use these feelings (e.g., irritation, protectiveness) to help them understand the masochistic patient's dynamics.

Therapists can also use their countertransference feelings as a gauge for recognizing transference experiences that are evoked in group members and employ them as a signal to ask the group members what they were feeling during a particular interaction (e.g., "As John was talking about his wife, what were you feeling?"). Therapists also can watch for additional nonverbal as well as verbal reactions in group members that can indicate transference reactions (e.g., looking out the window, fidgeting), and ask members about their feelings when it seems appropriate to do so.

As discussed in Chapter 9, several transference and

countertransference reactions are quite common in working with masochistic personalities. These reactions include (a) overidentifying with the masochist's suffering, leading to feeling frustrated, helpless, or inadequate; (b) acting out the inducement to rescue or persecute the masochist as part of masochistic triangulation or projective identification; (c) feeling grateful as a result of projective identifications of ingratiation; and (d) feeling guilt as a result of masochistic manipulation (e.g., "After all I've done for you, how could you not do this for me?"). In group psychotherapy, it is important to discuss these types of reactions in group members (as well as in oneself) to help masochistic patients gain insight about particular dynamics and their interpersonal consequences.

HOW DIFFERENT PERSONALITIES TYPICALLY INTERACT WITH MASOCHISTIC PATIENTS IN GROUP PSYCHOTHERAPY

The authors have recommended that the therapy group best suited for the treatment of masochistic personalities be one that excludes patients with more extreme borderline personality organizations (Kernberg 1975) and includes a variety of other personality styles who can serve as transferential objects and stimulus cues for the masochistic patient. We now discuss the typical relationship patterns that masochistic personalities can have with other personality types and how the therapist may intervene in order to help create the curative factors related to increased insight and corrective relationships. Briefly, we examine the relationship patterns developed between masochists and other patients with obsessive-compulsive, narcissistic, paranoid, hysterical, and borderline tendencies.

Masochistic Patients' Interactions with Patients Who Have Obsessive Tendencies

Masochists often confuse an obsessive's need to do things the right way according to the demands of their excessively harsh superegos with narcissism and thus tend to feel shamed, defend themselves, and get involved in subtle power struggles with obsessive group members. Masochists' controlling behavior is often a defensive means of protecting themselves from object loss while obsessive-compulsive patients have more of a need to control things to maintain a sense of order. Both are trying to attain or protect a sense of internal security.

For example, masochistic patients may interpret obsessive patients' rational problem solving approaches to life as a devaluation and feel hurt and misunderstood. Obsessives may interpret masochists' frequent helpful behavior as controlling rather than as an effort to make a connection with them. They may thus respond to the masochist with irritation causing him or her to feel criticized and rejected. Group therapy can help patients understand the other's underlying motives and their own transferential misinterpretations.

Masochistic Patients' Interactions with Patients with Narcissistic Tendencies

Masochists often feel particularly drawn to narcissistic individuals, idealizing and adoring them only to feel used and abused at some point over the narcissistic individual's devaluing and distancing tendencies. Masochists generally want the approval of the narcissist, to win him or her over as the patient could not win the approval of the predominantly critical parent. Masochists, however, are angry at having to work so hard for such meager approval and thus at times do things to irritate narcissists, provoking them into behaving badly or passively expressing their own dissatisfaction. This dynamic is usually unconsciously driven and consciously denied by masochists, who are typically surprised that anyone would be irritated with them when they are trying so hard to help and please other people. Their surprise is often a clue to the therapist that this interpersonal sequence reflects a microcosm of their relationships outside of group.

For example, one masochistic patient continually asked a narcissistic patient what the narcissistic patient was thinking when she was quiet. The narcissist found the masochist's behavior intrusive and annoying and thus generally responded with criticism, which at one level satisfied the masochist's view of the world as a harsh place and at another level perplexed him as he felt that he was only expressing interest and concern.

In addition, masochists often get into pursuer-distancer dynamics with narcissists. In the last example, the more intrusive the masochistic patient became, the more withdrawn and critical the narcissistic patient acted.

Masochistic Patients' Interactions with Patients with Paranoid Tendencies

The masochist's chronic helping often frightens individuals with paranoid tendencies. The masochist then tends to overpersonalize the paranoid's suspiciousness and responds by feeling hurt and unappreciated. The paranoid thus experiences the masochist as intrusive or pushy and presuming a relationship that they do not yet have. The masochist experiences the paranoid as ungrateful and hard to please.

For example, one masochistic patient offered to give a paranoid patient a hug and the paranoid patient pushed her away. The masochistic patient did this in spite of the paranoid patient's having been clear with the group about being uncomfortable with physical contact and especially with affection. It was important to help the masochist understand how she neglected to attend to the paranoid patient's signals.

Nydes (1963) formulated a polarity between the masochistic and paranoid characters regarding power and love (see Chapter 11). The paranoid's power operation is a kind of counterattack against an assumed intruder or accuser. Frequently the effect is to provoke the punishment against which he or she was supposedly defending him- or herself. The therapist can thus often observe both pursuer-distancer dynamics and power struggles between paranoid and masochistic patients in which each sees the other as the persecutor. The paranoid and masochist frequently argue about who is really the victim and who is persecuting whom.

Masochistic Patients' Interactions with Patients with Schizoid Tendencies

Masochists often feel rejected by schizoid patients. As with paranoid patients, schizoid patients often experience masochists as intrusive. Masochists, in turn, tend to project onto schizoids that they are being critical and rejecting when they are simply withdrawn as a self-protective mechanism. However, unlike paranoid and narcissistic patients, the schizoid patient has a need–fear dilemma. He or she thus welcomes (as well as fears) the masochist's advances, giving the masochist mixed messages. This can recapitulate the type of intermittent reinforcement that the masochist experienced in his or her family of origin.

Masochistic Patients' Interactions with Patients with Hysterical Tendencies

As with other group members with masochistic dynamics, masochists can feel competitive with group members who manifest hysterical tendencies. Both personality types attempt to draw the attention of others, albeit through different mechanisms. Masochists try to earn attention through excessive giving, while hysterics try to win attention through being charming and entertaining and making emotional displays. The masochist can feel jealous and resentful of the hysteric's ability to gain attention without appearing to have to work so hard to earn it.

In addition, masochists often recognize partial truths about the hysteric and based on those clues, project their own compliance and hypocrisy onto him or her. Masochists have negative reactions to the hysteric's pseudo-emotionality for several reasons. They experience the hysteric as inauthentic and believe that they can't express their real selves with him or her. In addition, they experience the hysteric's compliments and general positive expressions as insincere. This is both a projection and a transference of the parent figure that was experienced as overtly positive, but having an underlying disregard for them. Thus, with the hysterical group member, it is important to help the masochist sort out his or her realistic perceptions from their transference and projections.

Masochistic Patients' Interactions with Patients with Borderline Tendencies

Masochists often have an initial attraction to individuals with borderline characteristics. Their desire to be needed is activated by individuals whose needs are so intense and immediate. This interaction satisfies the masochist's deep yearning to secure a relationship by making oneself indispensable. With a borderline, this unstated relationship agreement comes at a high price. Borderlines are even more sensitive to disappointment than masochists and they are more rageful and vengeful in their response.

Thus, when masochists disappoint the borderline patient, the borderline may become furious and see the masochist as "all bad," which recapitulates the masochist's family of origin. However, if patients are selected for group with only mild borderline tendencies rather than a severe borderline disorder, there is also an opportunity for both patients to learn and grow from their experiences with each other.

This chapter has reviewed an approach to treating masochistic patients in an interactional psychotherapy group based upon principles of object relations therapy. As in individual object relations therapy, treatment is based upon furthering the patient's insight and providing him or her with a corrective interpersonal experience. In group psychotherapy, however, there are a greater amount of transference objects and more opportunities for corrective relationship experiences. Furthermore, when the masochistic character is very ingrained, feedback from several group members can have the advantage of confronting more rigid defenses.

14

Conclusion

We have presented an object relations-based conceptualization of the diagnosis and treatment of the preneurotic masochistic personality, the first detailed conceptualization of preneurotic masochism that has yet been attempted to our knowledge. The only previously published works in this area have been exceptionally brief. Althea Horner's (1979) initial introduction of the concept of preneurotic ego/object relations comprised only one page in her book *Object Relations and the Developing Ego in Therapy*. Varga's (1985) article, which connected preneurotic ego/object relations development to masochistic character pathology, was cogent but also very brief.

In expanding extensively on the previously brief diagnostic conceptualizations of preneurotic masochism, this book has furnished a detailed object relations model of psychotherapy that (a) offers greater specificity to the concept of providing patients with a corrective interpersonal experience than previously described by other theorists (e.g., Fairbairn, Sullivan), (b) takes developmental deficits and structural change into account more than does Benjamin's SASB model, (c) discusses proactive strategies for dealing with particular character disorders more than does Cashdan's model, and (d) further expands upon the therapeutic strategies for remediating developmental deficits as articulated by Horner (1979, 1991) .

We have proposed that the preneurotic masochistic personality represents a self-defeating way of loving and individuating that reflects a disturbance in object relations/ego development. This disturbance is fixated at the level of separation-individuation, which Mahler and colleagues (1975) labeled "on the way to object constancy." In this context, preneurotic masochism signifies neither a sexual disorder nor the deriving of pleasure from pain, but rather a disturbance in object relations/ego development that has as its hallmark a failure to complete transmuting internalizations of realistic maternal functions due to intense ambivalence toward the maternal object. This failure of completion leaves masochists psychologically insecure and overreliant upon others to regulate their narcissistic equilibrium. They are also left with the unconscious belief that they must endure great suffering in order to maintain their designated security relationships.

We have described in detail the clinical manifestations of preneurotic masochism, the structural and defensive hallmarks of this disorder, and the etiological factors involved in its development. The hallmarks of preneurotic masochism include a propensity to (a) employ one variant or another of masochistic splitting, which reflects the masochist's defensive style of "internalizing the burden of badness" (Fairbairn 1954); (b) engage in anxious attachments with security objects who predominantly and/or erratically give non-love; (c) exhibit a distinct vulnerability to depression and excessive dependence upon a somewhat idealized other in order to stabilize internal security and self-esteem due to incomplete internalizations of maternal functions; and (d) manifest strivings for autonomy/individuation through help-rejecting passive-aggressiveness, assuming dominant caretaking roles, and subtle provocation that leads to power struggles. The preneurotic masochist's incomplete transmuting internalizations of realistic, maternal functions are related to structural issues such as identity formation, self-esteem, object attachment, and strivings for individuation. Masochistic attitudes and behaviors are designed to enable individuals to maintain their attachment to the parental ego ideal or critical internal object from whom they are unable to completely separate due to intense and unresolved ambivalence.

We have differentiated masochism structured at the neurotic and borderline levels of ego/object relations from masochism structured at the preneurotic level, as well as preneurotic masochism from paranoid, narcissistic, obsessive-compulsive, hysteroid borderline, and hysterical disorders. While many clients present with mixed personality disorders, we posit that being able to differentiate various character disorders and levels of ego/object relations structure will help therapists more effectively plan and execute treatment strategies as well as constructively anticipate and use countertransference feelings.

Outlined are typical countertransference reactions and strategies designed to help therapists disengage from and constructively use their reactions to further the therapeutic process. Tolerating and empathizing with the masochist's sense of helplessness and victimization can evoke rescuing efforts, frustrations, and discomfort in the most experienced therapist. To the extent that therapists, themselves, have masochistic tendencies, they are especially vulnerable to overidentification with the masochistic process. This identification often needs to be addressed in supervision or consultation in order for the therapist to effectively remain in a nonreactive stance with these patients.

We have discussed psychotherapeutic strategies designed to heal masochistic wounds, prominent among which is the development of a corrective interpersonal relationship that helps the patient complete internalizations of self-regulatory functions. Since the internalizations of these functions can be realized only through the activation of the masochist's true self, the therapist needs to help masochists discern when they are presenting their adaptive false-self, and help them discover ways to create the safety needed to bring their true selves into the therapy hour. In general, masochists need a genuine relationship in which the therapist behaves in a nonreactive, sincere, empathic, dependable manner and supports the patient's autonomy, observing ego, and self-empowerment. This process often entails helping masochists internalize self-regulatory functions that increase their capacity to tolerate separations and loss and to create viable options to their typical either/or approach to life. We concluded by extending this model to couples and group treatment.

This work attempts to offer a better understanding of the complex and adaptive functions of masochistic behavior (e.g., individuative strivings, anxious attachment), instead of simplifying its meaning as the derivation of sexual or general pleasure from painful experiences. We hope that the expansion of this construct enables therapists to provide more individually tailored effective treatment to patients who struggle with these issues. We would also be pleased if our efforts lead to a diminishing of the pejorative and gender-biased associations with the term *masochism*, so that it once again becomes a viable construct for clinicians and part of our commonly used psychiatric nomenclature.

References

Ables, B. S., and Brandsma, J. M. (1977). *Therapy for Couples.* San Francisco: Jossey-Bass.

Ainsworth, M. D., Bell, S. M., and Stayton, D. J. (1969). Individual differences in strange situation behavior of one year old. In *The Origins of Human Social Behavior*, ed. H. R. Schaffer. New York: Academic Press, 1946.

Alexander, F., and French, T. M. (1946). *Psychoanalytic Therapy.* New York: Ronald Press.

American Psychiatric Association. (1987). *Diagnostic and Statistical Manual of Mental Disorders*, 3rd ed., rev. Washington, DC: APA

_____ (1994). *Diagnostic and Statistical Manual of Mental Disorders*, 4th ed. Washington, DC: APA.

Aronson, T. (1989). Paranoia and narcissism. *Psychoanalytic Review* 76(3): 329–351.

Asch, S. S. (1988). The analytic concepts of masochism: a

re-evaluation. In *Masochism: Current Psychoanalytic Perspectives*, ed. R. A. Glick and D. I. Meyers. Hillsdale, N J: Analytic Press.

Avery, N. D. (1977). Sadomasochism: a defense against object loss. *Psychoanalytic Review* 64(1):101–109.

Azrin, N. H., and Holz, W. C. (1966). Punishment. In *Operant Behavior: Areas of Research and Application*, ed. W. K. Honig. New York: Appelton, Century, Croft.

Bak, R. C. (1946). Masochism and paranoia. *Psychoanalytic Quarterly* 15:285–301.

Bardwick, J. (1991). *Psychology of Women: A Study of Bio-Cultural Conflicts*. New York: Harper & Row.

Barnett, J. (1971). Narcissism and dependency in the obsessional hysterical marriage. *Family Process* 10:75–83.

Beattie, M. (1987). *Codependent No More*. New York: Hazeldon Foundation.

Beck, A. (1967). *Depression*. New York: Harper & Row.

Beier, E. G. (1966). *The Silent Language of Psychotherapy: Social Reinforcement of Unconscious Processes*. Chicago: Aldine.

Beardslee, W. (1989). The role of self-understanding in resilient individuals. The development of a perspective. *American Journal of Orthopsychiatry* 59(2): 266–278.

Benjamin, L. S. (1979). Structural analysis of differential failure. Use of structural analysis of social behavior (SASB) and Markov chains to study dyadic interactions. *Journal of Abnormal Psychology* 88:303–319.

———— (1993). *Interpersonal Diagnosis and Treatment of Personality Disorders*. New York: Guilford.

Bergler, E. (1961). *Curable and Incurable Neurosis*. New York: Liveright.

Berliner, B. (1947). On some psychodynamics of masochism. *Psychoanalytic Quarterly* 16(4):459–471.

_____ (1958). The role of object relations in moral masoch-ism. *Psychoanalytic Quarterly* 27:38–56.

Bernstein, L. (1957). The role of object relations in moral masochism. *Psychoanalytic Quarterly* 26:358–377.

Bieber, I. (1966). Sadism and masochism. In *American Handbook of Psychiatry*, vol. 3, ed. S. Arieti. New York: Basic Books.

Blum, H.P. (1977). Masochism, the ego ideal and psychology of women. *Journal of the American Psychoanalytic Association* 24:157–191.

Bowlby, J. (1973). *Attachment and Loss*. New York: Basic Books.

Brennan, M. (1952). On teasing and being teased; and the problems of moral masochism. *Psychoanalytic Study of the Child* 7:264–285. New York: International Universities Press.

Brenner, C. (1959). The masochistic character: genesis and treatment. *Journal of the American Psychoanalytic Association* 7:197–226.

Bromberg, W. (1955). Maternal influences in the development of moral masochism. *American Journal of Orthopsychiatry* 25:802–812.

Caplan, P. J. (1984). The myth of women's masochism. *American Psychologist* 39:130–139.

Cashdan, S. (1988). *Object Relations Therapy*.New York: W.W. Norton.

Chessick, R. D. (1983). Problems in the intensive psychotherapy of the borderline patient. *Dynamic Psychotherapy* 1:20–32.

Clance, P. R., and Imes, S. A. (1978). The impostor phenomena in high achieving women: dynamics and therapeutic intervention. *Psychotherapy: Theory, Research, and Practice* 15(3):241–247.

Cooper, A. M. (1988). The narcissistic-masochistic character. In *Masochism: Current Psychoanalytic Perspectives*, ed. R. A. Glick and D. I. Meyers. Hillsdale, NJ: Analytic Press.

Cooper, A. M., and Fischer, N. (1981). Masochism: current concepts. *Journal of American Psychoanalytic Association* 29:673–688.

Dolan, R., Arnkoff, P., and Glass, C. (1993). Client's attachment style and the therapist's interpersonal stance. *Psychotherapy* 30(3): 408–412.

Deutsch, H. (1944). *Psychology of Women.* London: Hogarth Press.

Dryden, W. (1991). *Therapist's Dilemmas.* London: Harper & Row.

Egeland, B., and Farber, F. (1985). Infant-mother attachment: factors related to its development and changes over time. *Child Development* 55(3): 753–771.

Erikson, E. (1950). *Childhood and Society.* New York: W.W. Norton.

Fairbairn, W. R. D. (1943). The repression and the return of bad objects. In *Psychoanalytic Studies of the Personality*, vol. 7. London: Routledge and Kegan Paul, 1981.

—— (1952). *Psychoanalytic Studies of the Personality*, vol. 7. London: Routledge and Kegan Paul.

—— (1954). *An Object Relations Theory of the Personality.* New York: Basic Books.

Fenichel, O. (1945). *The Psychoanalytic Theory of Neurosis.* New York: W.W. Norton.

Fisher, A. E. (1955). *The Effects of Differential Early Treatment on the Social and Exploratory Behavior of Puppies.* Unpublished doctoral dissertation, Pennsylvania State University.

Forward, S. (1986). *Men Who Hate Women and the Women Who Love Them.* New York: Bantam Books.

Franklin, D. (1987). The politics of masochism. *Psychology Today* 21:52–57.

Freud, S. (1905). Three essays on the theory of sexuality. *Standard Edition* 7:125–245.

―――― (1919). A child is beaten. *Standard Edition* 18:8–64.

―――― (1924). The economic problem of masochism. *Standard Edition* 19:157–170.

Ganzarain, R. (1992). Introduction to object relations group psychotherapy. *International Journal of Group Psychotherapy* 42:205–223.

Gear, M. C., Hill, M. A., and Liendo, E. C. (1983). *Working Through Narcissism: Treating Its Sadomasochistic Structure*. New York: Jason Aronson.

Gear, M. C., and Liendo, E. C. (1981). *Therapie Psycho-analytique de la Famille*. Paris: Dunod.

Gear, M. C., Liendo, E. C., and Scott, L. (1981). Metapsychology of sadism and masochism. *Psychoanalytic Contemporary Thought* 14:207–250.

Gero, G. (1962). Sadism, masochism and aggression: their role in symptom formation. *Psychoanalytic Quarterly* 31:31–41.

Glick, R. A., and Meyers, D. I., eds. (1988). *Masochism: Current Psychoanalytic Perspectives*. Hillsdale, NJ: Analytic Press.

Glickauf-Hughes, C. (1994). Dynamics and treatment of the narcissistic-masochistic couple. *Psychoanalysis and Psychotherapy* 11(1):32–44.

Glickauf-Hughes, C., and Wells, M. (1991). Current conceptualizations on masochism: genesis and object relations. *American Journal of Psychotherapy* 45(1):53–68.

Glickauf-Hughes, C., and Wells, M. (In press). Separation and idealization in the masochistic personality. *Issues in Psychoanalytic Psychology*.

Glickauf-Hughes, C., Wells, M., and Genirberg, R. (1987). Psychotherapy of gifted students with narcissistic dynamics. *Journal of College Student Psychotherapy* 1:99–115.

Grand, H. G. (1973). The masochistic defense of the double magic: its relationship to imposture. *International Journal of Psycho-Analysis* 54: 445–454.

Greenberg, J. R., and Mitchell, S. A. (1983). *Object Relations in Psychoanalytic Theory*. Cambridge, MA: Harvard University Press.

Greenson, R. (1967). *The Techniques and Practice of Psychoanalysis*, vol. 1. New York: International Universities Press.

Grief, A. C. (1985). Masochism and the therapist. *Psychoanalytic Review* 72(3): 491–501.

Grotnick, I. (1982). The problem of treating an intensely suffering patient: to gratify or frustrate. *Psychoanalytic Review* 69(4):487–493.

Grotstein, J. S. (1981). *Splitting and Projective Identification*. New York: Jason Aronson.

Guntrip, H. (1961). *Personality Structure and Human Interaction*. New York: International Universities Press.

—— (1969). *Schizoid Phenomena, Object Relations and the Self*. New York: International Universities Press.

Haaken, J., and Schlaps, A. (1991). Incest resolution therapy and the objectification of sexual abuse. *Psychotherapy: Theory, Research, and Practice* 28(1): 39–47.

Hamilton, G. (1988). *Self and Others: Object Relations Theory in Practice*. Northvale, N.J.: Jason Aronson.

Hedges, L. E. (1983). *Listening Perspectives in Psychotherapy*. New York: Jason Aronson.

Horner, A. (1979). *Object Relations and the Developing Ego in Therapy*. New York: Jason Aronson.

—— (1991). *Psychoanalytic Object Relations Therapy*. Northvale, N.J.: Jason Aronson.

Horney, K. (1939). *Neurosis and Human Growth*. New York: W. W. Norton.

Jacobs, T. (1993). *On beginnings: alliances, misalliances, and the interplay of transferences in the opening phase.* Paper presented at the American Psychoanalytic Association Seminar for Clinicians.

Johnson, S. (1985). *Characterological Transformation.* New York: W.W. Norton.

_____ (1987). *Humanizing the Narcissistic Style.* New York: W. W. Norton.

Jordan, J. (1993). Relational models of development: clinical implications. *The Psychotherapy Bulletin* 28(3): 22–36.

Kernberg, O. (1968). The treatment of patients with borderline personality organizations. *International Journal of Psycho-Analysis* 49: 600–619.

_____ (1974). Forms and transformations of narcissism. *Journal of American Psychoanalytic Association* 14:243–272.

_____ (1975). *Borderline Conditions and Pathological Narcissism.* New York: Jason Aronson.

_____ (1976). *Object Relations Theory and Clinical Psychoanalysis.* New York: Jason Aronson.

_____ (1988). Clinical dimensions of masochism. In *Masochism: Current Psychoanalytic Perspectives*, ed. R. A. Glick, and D. L. Meyers, pp. 61–80. Hillsdale, NJ: Analytic Press,

Klein, M. (1935). A contribution to the psychogenesis of manic-depressive states. *Contributions to Psychoanalysis, 1921–1925*, ed. M. Klein. New York: McGraw-Hill, 1964.

Klimek, D. (1979). *Beneath Mate Selection and Marriage: The Unconscious Motives in Human Pairing.* New York: Van Nostrand Reinhold.

Kohut, H. (1971). *The Analysis of the Self.* New York: International Universities Press.

_____ (1977). *The Restoration of the Self.* New York: International Universities Press.

Krafft-Ebing, R. F. (1895). *Psychopathia Sexualis.* London: F. A. Davis.

Krohn, A. (1978). *Hysteria: The Elusive Neurosis.* New York: International Universities Press.

Lachkar, J. (1985). Narcissistic-borderline couples: theoretical implications for treatment. *Dynamic Psychotherapy* 2:109–125.

Lasch, C. (1978). *The Culture of Narcissism.* New York: W. W. Norton.

Lazarus, A. (1993). Tailoring the therapeutic relationship or being an authentic chameleon. *Psychotherapy* 30(3):404–407.

Leary, T. (1957). *Interpersonal Diagnosis of Personality.* New York: Ronald.

Lieberman, M. (1982). The effect of social supports on response to stress. In *Handbook of Stress: Theoretical and Clinical Aspects*, ed. L. Goldberger, and S. Breznitz. New York: Free Press.

Light, N. (1974). The "chronic helper" in group therapy. *Perspectives in Psychiatric Care* 12(3):129–134.

Mahler, M. S., Pine, F., and Bergman, A. (1975). *The Psychological Birth of the Human Infant: Symbiosis and Individuation.* New York: Basic Books.

Mahrer, A. (1993). The experiential relationship: Is it all purpose or is it tailored to the individual client? *Psychotherapy* 30(3):413–416.

Martin, P., and Bird, H. (1959). A marriage pattern: the "lovesick" wife and the "cold, sick" husband. *Psychiatry: Journal of the Study of Interpersonal Process* 22: 245–254.

Masterson, J. F. (1981). *The Narcissistic and Borderline Disorders: An Integrated Developmental Approach.* New York: Brunner/Mazel.

McCormack, C. (1984). The borderline/schizoid marriage: the holding environment as an essential treatment construct. *Journal of Marriage and Family Therapy* 15: 299–309.

Meissner, W.W. (1978). *The Paranoid Process.* New York: Jason Aronson.

_____ (1989). A note on psychoanalytic facts. *Psychoanalytic Inquiry* 9(2):193–219.

Menaker, E. (1953). Masochism—a defensive reaction of the ego. *Psychoanalytic Quarterly* 22:205–220.

Meyers, H. (1988). A consideration of treatment techniques in relation to the functions of masochism. In *Masochism—Current Psychoanalytic Perspectives*, ed. R. Glick, and D. Meyers. Hillsdale, NJ: Analytic Press.

Miller, A. (1981). *The Drama of the Gifted Child.* New York: Basic Books.

Minuchin, S., Montalvo, B., Guerney, B., et al. (1967). *Families of the Slums: An Exploration of Their Structure and Treatment.* New York: Basic Books.

Mollinger, R. N. (1982). Sadomasochism and developmental states. *Psychiatric Review* 69:379–389.

Mueller, W., and Aniskiewicz, A. (1986). *Psychotherapeutic Intervention in Hysterical Disorders.* Northvale, NJ: Jason Aronson.

Norcross, J. (1993). Tailoring relational stances to clients' needs: an introduction. *Psychotherapy* 30:402–403.

Norwood, R. (1985). *Women Who Love Too Much.* Los Angeles: Jeremy Tarcher.

Nydes, J. (1963). The paranoid-masochistic character. *Psychoanalytic Review* 50:55–91.

Ogden, T. H. (1979). *Projective Identification and Psychotherapeutic Technique.* New York: Jason Aronson.

Panken, S. (1983). *The Joy of Suffering.* New York: Jason Aronson.

Peck, S. (1978). *The Road Less Traveled: A New Psychology of Love, Spiritual Values and Growth.* New York: Simon & Schuster.

Pine, F. (1993). A contribution to the analysis of the psychoanalytic process. *Psychoanalytic Quarterly* 2:185–205.

Rapaport, D. (1951). The conceptual model of psychoanalysis. *Journal of Personality*, 20:56–81.

Reich, W. (1933). *Character Analysis*. New York: Simon & Schuster.

Reik, T. (1941). *Masochism in Modern Man*. New York: Farrar and Rinehart.

Renik, O. (1993). Countertransference enactment and the psychoanalytic process. In *Psychic Structure and Psychic Change*, ed. M. Horowitz, O. Kernberg, and E. Weinshel. New York: International Universities Press.

Rogers, C. (1965). *On Becoming a Person*. Boston: Houghton Mifflin.

Rucker, H. (1968). *Transference and Countertransference*. New York: International Universities Press.

Rutter, M. (1986). Meyerian psychology, personality disorders and the role of life experiences. *American Journal of Psychiatry* 13:1077–1087.

Salzman, L. (1980). *Treatment of the Obsessive Personality*. New York: Jason Aronson.

Salzman, L., and Thaler, F. M. (1981). Obsessive-compulsive personality disorders: a review of the literature. *American Journal of Psychiatry* 138(3): 286–296.

Schwartzman, G. (1984). Narcissistic transferences: implications for couples. *Dynamic Psychotherapy* 2:5–13.

Seiden, H.M. (1989). The narcissistic counterpart. *Psychoanalytic Review* 76(1):67–81.

Selwyn, L. (1988). The use of group therapy to modify the harsh superego of patients and the group therapist. *Issues in Ego Psychology* 11(1): 43–57.

Shapiro, D. (1965). *Neurotic Styles*. New York: Basic Books.

Shapiro, S. (1989). The provocative masochistic patient: an intersubjective approach to treatment. *Bulletin of the Menninger Clinic* 4: 319–331.

Slipp, S. (1984). *Object Relations: A Dynamic Bridge Between Individual and Family Treatment.* New York: Jason Aronson.

Smaldino, C. (1984). Out from under: countertransference in the treatment of the masochistic adolescent youngster. *Child and Adolescent Social Work Journal* 1:168–180.

Smirnoff, V. (1969). The masochistic contract. *International Journal of Psycho-Analysis* 50:665–671.

Solomon, M. F. (1985). Treatment of narcissistic and borderline disorders in marital therapy: suggestions towards an enhanced therapeutic approach. *Clinical Social Work Journal* 13:141–156.

_____ (1988). Self psychology and marital relations. *International Journal of Family Psychiatry* 9:211–226.

Speers, R. W., and Marter, D. C. (1980). Overseparation and underindividuation of the pseudo-mature child. In *Rapprochement: Critical Subphase of Separation-Individuation*, ed. R. Lax, S. Bach, and J. A. Burland, pp. 457–478. New York: Jason Aronson.

Stolorow, R. D. (1975). The narcissistic function of masochism (and sadism). *International Journal of Psycho-Analysis* 56:441–448.

Stolorow, R. D., and Lachman, F. M. (1980). *Psychoanalysis of Developmental Arrests: Theory and Treatment.* New York: International Universities Press.

Sullivan, H. S. (1940). *Concepts of Modern Psychiatry.* New York: W.W. Norton

_____ (1953). *The Interpersonal Theory of Psychiatry.* New York: W.W. Norton.

Varga, M. P. (1985). An object relations perspective on dealing with depressive masochistic character resistances. *Issues in Ego Psychology* 8(1):59–62.

Weiss, J. (1993). *How Psychotherapy Works.* New York: Guilford.

Wells, M., and Glickauf-Hughes, C. (1986). Techniques for establishing object constancy in borderline clients. *Psychotherapy: Theory, Research, and Practice* 23(3):460–468.

—— (1993). A psychodynamic object relations model for differential diagnosis. *Psychotherapy Bulletin* 28(3):41–48.

Wells, M., Glickauf-Hughes, C., and Buzzell, V. (1990). Treating obsessive-compulsives in psychodynamic-interpersonal group therapy. *Psychotherapy: Theory, Research and Practice*

Willi, J. (1982). *Couples in Collusion.* New York: Jason Aronson and Hunter House.

Winnicott, D. W. (1958). *Through Pediatrics to Psychoanalysis.* London: Hogarth.

—— (1965). *The Maturational Process and the Facilitating Environment.* New York: International Universities Press.

Woititz, J. (1983). *Adult Children of Alcoholics.* Deerfield Beach, FL: Health Communications.

Yalom, I. (1975). *Theory and Practice of Group Psychotherapy.* New York: Basic Books.

Young, D. M., and Beier, E. G. (1982). Being asocial in social places: giving the client a new experience. In *Handbook of Interpersonal Psychotherapy*, ed. J. C. Anchin, and D. J. Kiesler. New York: Pergamon Press.

Young, G. H., and Gerson, S. (1991). New psychoanalytic perspectives on masochism and spouse abuse. *Psychotherapy: Theory, Research, and Practice* 28(1): 30–37.

Index